What makes the words we speak mean what they do? Possible-worlds semantics articulates the view that the meanings of words contribute to determining, for each sentence, which possible worlds would make the sentence true, and which would make it false. M. J. Cresswell argues that the non-semantic facts on which such semantic facts supervene are facts about the causal interactions between the linguistic behaviour of speakers and the facts in the world that they are speaking about, and that the kind of causation involved is best analysed using David Lewis's account of causation in terms of counterfactuals. Although philosophers have worked on the question of the connection between meaning and linguistic behaviour, it has mostly been without regard to the work done in possible-worlds semantics, and *Language in the world* is the first book-length examination of this problem.

T0382159

CAMBRIDGE STUDIES IN PHILOSOPHY

Language in the world

CAMBRIDGE STUDIES IN PHILOSOPHY

General editor ERNEST SOSA

Advisory editors J. E. J. ALTHAM, SIMON BLACKBURN,
GILBERT HARMAN, MARTIN HOLLIS, FRANK JACKSON,
WILLIAM G. LYCAN, JOHN PERRY,
SYDNEY SHOEMAKER, BARRY STROUD

RECENT TITLES

Language in the world

A PHILOSOPHICAL ENQUIRY

M. J. Cresswell

Professor of Philosophy
Victoria University of Wellington

CAMBRIDGE
UNIVERSITY PRESS

CAMBRIDGE UNIVERSITY PRESS
Cambridge, New York, Melbourne, Madrid, Cape Town, Singapore, São Paulo

Cambridge University Press
The Edinburgh Building, Cambridge CB2 8RU, UK

Published in the United States of America by Cambridge University Press, New York

www.cambridge.org
Information on this title: www.cambridge.org/9780521445627

© Cambridge University Press 1994

First published 1994
This digitally printed version 2007

A catalogue record for this publication is available from the British Library

ISBN 978-0-521-44562-7 hardback
ISBN 978-0-521-04621-3 paperback

Contents

Preface

This book was begun in January 1991, initially as a set of course notes for a graduate course in the philosophy of language which I taught in the fall semester of 1991 at the University of Massachusetts at Amherst. In addition to my UMass students, Adriane, Bruce, Julie, David, and others, whose names appear in these pages, my lectures were attended by Lynne Baker, Ed Gettier, Phil Bricker and Barbara Partee, all of whom made valuable comments of which some even made it into the text.

A draft of the book was written up in the first three months of 1992 in the comfortable and welcome environment of the Centre for Cognitive Science at the University of Edinburgh, and some of the material was presented in a seminar there. Many people in Edinburgh made those months profitable. In particular regular sessions with Robin Cooper were especially helpful and encouraging. I would like to thank the Science and Engineering Research Council for financial support in Edinburgh.

In April of 1992 I moved to Cambridge and enjoyed the experience of living in college for the Easter term. I would express my heartfelt thanks to the Master and Fellows of St John's College for the Visiting Overseas Scholarship that I held that term. I am also grateful to Hugh Mellor and the other philosophers in Cambridge for the opportunity to give six lectures on the material in this book and for the willingness of my colleagues to engage in philosophical discussion.

Finally, to the Victoria University of Wellington for giving me 1992 as a sabbatical year, and to my department for doing without me for eighteen months, I express sincere thanks. I trust that the existence of this book demonstrates that I did not spend all my time riding trains. Our department secretary, Debbie Luyinda, put most of the material into the word processor so that I could spend my time playing with it. Thank you.

Cambridge
May 1992

Introduction

We know a lot about the semantic structure of natural language. If you think that semantics is about the connection between linguistic entities, words, sentences and such, and non-linguistic entities, things 'in the world', then the way to do semantics will be to specify the linguistic entities, then specify the 'things in the world' which are to be their meanings, and then connect up the two. Chapters 1 and 2 illustrate this by setting out in detail a very simple formal language together with its semantics. This semantics allows us to address the philosophical issues with a particular example in mind. (These chapters can be omitted by those who already have a background in formal semantics.) The kind of semantic theory set out is what is called possible-worlds semantics, and is based on the idea that the meaning of a sentence is the conditions under which it is true, and that these conditions are simply the class of possible worlds in which the sentence is true.

Many years ago, in Cresswell 1978, I defended this approach to semantics by arguing that speakers of a language know the truth conditions of the sentences they utter, and that it is this knowledge which constitutes their semantic competence. It was David Lewis who, when I gave this talk at Princeton in 1975, convinced me that there was a problem. I had argued that to know meaning is to know truth conditions. Lewis asked what it is to know truth conditions. If an interpretation to a language is a pairing of expressions with their meanings then the fact that certain expressions are paired with certain meanings will be a *mathematical* (or logical) fact. But it is obvious that someone who knows no English is not suffering a deficiency of mathematical knowledge. The empirical fact is that a certain formal structure correctly models the behaviour of a linguistic population in ways in which alternative structures do not. Thus an interpretation in which the word **horse** refers to horses is correct in a sense in which an interpretation in which **horse** refers to lobsters is wrong.

1

So the question becomes: What is it to model correctly the linguistic behaviour of a population? Lewis 1975 has produced one answer, and his answer is discussed in chapter 7 of this book. That answer links the semantics of languages with the content of propositional attitudes, specifically with belief and desire. In Cresswell 1978 my reply to the comment that I did not say what it was for certain sentences to have the truth conditions they do, was that such facts exist even if we cannot say what they are. In Cresswell 1982, I took this a little further. I argued that although semantic facts may supervene on psychological (and presumably social) facts, yet there may be no way of *reducing* semantic facts to other kinds of facts. If this is so then semantics must be taken as autonomous in the sense that any semantic theory simply has to take as primitive and not further analysable that thus and such a sentence has thus and such truth conditions in the language of a linguistic population. (This seems to me the conclusion that Schiffer 1987 *ought* to have drawn.)

Although you may not be able to give any reductive analysis of semantic facts in non-semantic terms – and this is the 'conclusion' I come to in chapter 10 – yet you should be able to say *something* about what it is that justifies semantic structures, and about why possible-worlds semantics has the plausibility it does. In chapters 3–5 I try to set the stage by adding to the possible-worlds framework already introduced via the interpretations to the language set out in chapters 1 and 2, language users and relations between them and their languages. Along the way I say something about the possible-worlds metaphysics that I presuppose. In chapter 6 I discuss Putnam's twin-earth example to see whether it really does cast doubt on possible-worlds semantics as Putnam seems to have thought. Chapter 7 discusses Lewis's attempt to analyse semantic facts in terms of propositional attitudes, and also looks at the discussion in Field 1972 of the view that Tarski shewed that semantic facts have an even simpler reductive analysis.

Whatever the details may be about exactly what kind of non-semantic facts constitute semantic facts or constitute the content of propositional attitudes, it seems pretty clear that in a broad sense they are facts about the causal interactions between the linguistic behaviour of speakers and the facts in the world that they are speaking about. In chapter 8 I argue that the kind of causation involved is best analysed using Lewis's account, in Lewis 1973b, of causation in terms of counterfactuals. If in turn you analyse counterfactuals as Lewis does in

2

Lewis 1973a, so that 'If α had been the case then so would β' is true in a possible world *w* iff β is true in the world most like *w* in which α is true, then by putting language users into the possible worlds used to model their language you have a very intuitive explanation of why possible-worlds semantics is so plausible.

Although chapter 8 argues that possible-worlds semantics is plausible because it models so well the causal relations between language users and the world, it does not attempt to give any specific account of just what more 'basic' facts constitute the fact that our words mean what they do or that our beliefs and desires have the content they do. Both David Lewis and Robert Stalnaker have argued that the way to naturalize content is via the role of beliefs and desires in an explanation of behaviour. Chapter 9 explores this proposal. While I produce no arguments to shew that you cannot achieve a reductive analysis of this content an examination of the explicit proposals on pp. 27–40 of Lewis 1986a and in chapter 1 of Stalnaker 1984 shews how problematic it is to get a viable account, and in my view makes it likely that there is no account to be had. Some of the issues I shall be discussing have been raised by authors concerned with the advocacy in Davidson 1967 of the use of the theory of truth in Tarski 1936. One of the claims made there is that a semantical theory for a language can be given without any need to refer to what the speakers of that language know or do. I myself find semantical discussions in this tradition somewhat obscure and so I will be raising the issues in the context of possible-worlds semantics. Since most semantics which is actually *done*, as opposed to being talked about, is done in the possible-worlds framework, a discussion within this framework will give us access to a large body of literature.

Chapter 10 tries to say why it might be that there is no account to be had of the relation between semantic content and the non-semantic facts on which the semantic facts supervene. The nature of the dependence might just be too complicated. But if it is too complicated how can we *know* semantic facts? And clearly we *do* know semantic facts. I suggest that we might have a capacity for recognizing complicated patterns of psychological, social and other facts which are too complicated for us to have a theory of. This certainly seems to happen in knowledge of our own mental states, and that knowledge feels very like our instant recognition of the meanings of utterances that we and others produce. If this is right then the fact that we cannot naturalize semantics is only to be expected, and semantics must proceed as an autonomous discipline with its own source of semantic facts, known to speakers, as its data.

1

A simple formal language

This book is concerned with what makes one interpretation of a language the correct one and another the wrong one. I will be discussing this problem in the context of possible-worlds semantics and so, in order to set the scene, and by way of introduction for those who have not come across possible-worlds semantics for natural languages, I shall, in the first two chapters, set out a simple fragment so that we can see what is going on.

I hope that most of you will have a familiarity with at least the language of the first-order predicate calculus. (sometimes called the lower predicate calculus or LPC). I shall set out here a simple version of this, but without quantifiers, which I can generalize to a language rich enough for the points I want to make. So here is a language $\mathcal{L}$.

Sentences or *well-formed formulae* of $\mathcal{L}$ are finite sequences of what are called *symbols*. Although, in logical languages, symbols are often represented by letters, it is best to think of them as corresponding to *words* in natural language rather than letters. The sentences of $\mathcal{L}$ are those allowed by the formation rules. The formation rules are sensitive to the *syntactic category* of each symbol. It is time to be specific.

(1) $\mathcal{L}$ contains a category of *names*. Let these be **Adriane, Bruce, Julie** and **David**.
(2) $\mathcal{L}$ contains a category of *predicates*. Let these be **runs, whistles** and **sees**.
(3) $\mathcal{L}$ contains a category of *sentential functors* (sometimes called connectives). Let these be **not, and** and **if**.
(4) $\mathcal{L}$ contains a left parenthesis, (, and a right parenthesis,).

Categories (2) and (3) may be further subdivided. For reasons which I will make clear **runs** and **whistles** are *one-place* predicates and **sees** is a two-place predicate. **not** is a one-place functor, while **and** and **if** are two-place functors.

The grammatically well-formed sequences, i.e. the *sentences*, of $\mathcal{L}$ are those and only those finite sequences of the symbols in (1)–(4) which satisfy the following *formation rules*:

FR1 If *a* is a name and *F* is a one-place predicate then *aF* is a sentence.

FR2 If *a* and *b* are names, not necessarily distinct, and *F* is a two-place predicate, then *aFb* is a sentence.

FR3 If α is a sentence then so are α*not*, (α *and* β) and (*if* αβ).

The sentences formed by FR1 and FR2 can be called atomic sentences. Those which involve FR3 can be called non-atomic or complex sentences. Those familiar with predicate logic will know that *aF* is more usually written as *Fa* and *aFb* as *Fab*. I have chosen to keep close to the order of the English sentences which the sentences of $\mathscr{L}$ are mimicking. For similar reasons I have put **not** after a sentence, rather than in front of it. FR1 and FR2 have been stated using what are often called *metalinguistic* (or sometimes *metalogical*) variables. FR1 is a statement in the (English) metalanguage in which we are talking about $\mathscr{L}$, and it is convenient to enrich it by the variables '*a*' '*b*' and '*F*' to stand for the names and predicates of $\mathscr{L}$. Since (1) and (2) are small we could replace FR1 and FR2 by a finite list of all the atomic formulae:

Adriane runs	*Bruce runs*
Adriane whistles	*Bruce whistles*
Julie runs	*David runs*
Julie whistles	*David whistles*
Adriane sees Adriane	
Adriane sees Bruce	
Adriane sees Julie	
Adriane sees David	

and so on

Even with (1) and (2) so small I hope that you can see that replacing FR1 and FR2 by a list is extremely cumbersome. Further it fails to capture the reason *why* these are all sentences of $\mathscr{L}$. Take

(5) **Adriane runs**

Adriane is a name and **runs** is a one-place predicate, so FR1 tells us that that is why (5) is a sentence. Replacing **runs** by the two-place predicate **sees** would give us

(6) **Adriane sees**

6

which is not a sentence of $\mathscr{L}$. (A digression is in order here. The distinction between one-place and two-place predicates of $\mathscr{L}$ is like the distinction between intransitive and transitive verbs in English. Unfortunately it is almost impossible to find an English transitive verb which cannot also be used intransitively. There are many good uses of (6), despite the fact that *sees* also occurs as a transitive verb. But in $\mathscr{L}$ (6) is not well formed.)

FR3 could have been stated in a more general form using metalogical variables. We would make a distinction between one-place functors and two-place functors. *not* would be a one-place functor, while *and* and *if* would be two-place functors. FR3 could then be expressed as

> FR3′ If δ is an n-place functor (n = 1,2) and $\alpha_1,...,\alpha_n$ are sentences, not necessarily distinct, then $(\delta\alpha_1...\alpha_n)$ is a sentence.

FR3′ is stated for generalization to arbitrary n-place functors. It does however ignore the difference, reflected in FR3, that *not* is placed after the sentence it applies to, *and* goes between the two sentences it links while *if* goes in front of them. You can either regard these features as syntactically unimportant, or you can further subcategorize the two-place functors. As an example of how the formation rules operate look at how to prove that the following is a sentence of $\mathscr{L}$.

(7) (*if Adriane runs not (Julie whistles and Bruce sees David*))

To shew that (7) is a sentence we first find its atomic parts. They are

(8) *Adriane runs*
(9) *Julie whistles*

and

(10) *Bruce sees David*

Examples (8) and (9) are sentences because they each consist of a name followed by a one-place predicate, while (10) is a sentence because it consists of a two-place predicate between two names. In (8) the a of FR1 is *Adriane* while the F is *runs*. In (9) a is *Julie* and F is *whistles*. In (10) the a and b of FR2 are, respectively *Bruce* and *David* and the F is *sees*.

Given (8) as a sentence, if (8) is the α of FR3 then FR3 tells us that

(11) *Adriane runs not*

is also a sentence. And given (9) and (10) as sentences then if (9) is the α of FR3 and (10) is β, FR3 tells that

(12) *(Julie whistles and Bruce sees David)*

is a sentence. Here the fact that α and β are metalinguistic *variables* is important. In getting (12) α referred to (9), while in getting (11) α referred to (8). We now use the fact that (11) and (12) are sentences to apply FR3 again. This time (11) is α and (12) is β; and the part of FR3 which applies is the last clause which says that two sentences (here (11) and (12)) preceded by *if* and enclosed in parentheses are a sentence.

I would like to mention an alternative description of the syntax of the predicates and functors of ℒ, a description which I hope will help later when I come to semantics. At a fairly intuitive level there seems to be a distinction between a name like **Adriane** and a predicate like **runs** along the following lines. The purpose of **Adriane** in ℒ is to name someone, to name Adriane. Adriane is one of the items in the domain of discourse that ℒ is talking about. (We are of course anticipating a little now – since so far ℒ has been introduced as an uninterpreted purely syntactic system. But if we believe, with Montague (1974, p.223 n. 2), that the interest of syntax is as a preliminary to semantics, we shall want it to reflect at least some semantic structure.) The purpose of **runs** on the other hand is to enable a sentence to say something about whatever it is that is named – viz. that that item runs. While the purpose of **Adriane** is just to be a name the purpose of **runs** is, so to speak, to form the sentence (8) out of that name. The purpose of a sentence, on the other hand, is just to say something – that Adriane runs. Looked at in this light it is names and sentences which are the basic syntactical categories, with predicates being symbols which make sentences out of names. In fact what are called *categorial languages* are based on precisely this assumption, and I shall now describe ℒ as a categorial language. The reason I am going to do this may at the moment appear technical, but in fact it will turn out to be philosophically important. This is because there are two competing dimensions of simplicity and complexity, even for a language like ℒ. In one dimension the symbols – names, predicates and functors – are all simple, while the sentences are all complex. In another dimension, in terms of their syntactic category, names and sentences are simple, while predicates and functors are complex. (And while in ℒ names are simple in both dimensions there are considerations which support assigning them a complex syntactic category.) When we come to look at theories of what

8

it is to understand a language the tension between these two dimensions turns out to be an important issue.

The system of syntactic categories needed for $\mathscr{L}$ is in fact very small. Take n and s as the basic categories of respectively name and sentence. Then a one-place predicate can be given category (s/n), for what it does is form a sentence (expression of category s) out of a name (expression of category n). A two-place predicate would be in category (s/nn) because it makes a sentence out of two names. The sentential connectives also belong to syntactic categories. *not* makes a sentence out of another sentence, and so is in category (s/s), while *and* and *if* each make a sentence out of two sentences and so are in category (s/ss). These are the only categories needed for $\mathscr{L}$, but it is not difficult to see that the representation of natural language suggests symbols in other categories. Here are one or two examples. Consider the word *nobody*.

(13) *nobody runs*

is a sentence whose structure might appear to be just like that of (8). But if so *nobody* would be a name, and we remember the trouble that Alice and the white king had in treating it as such. In logic *nobody* would be represented by a negated existential quantifier and would involve bound individual variables. For present purposes the addition of individual variables to $\mathscr{L}$ is an unnecessary complication. From a categorial point of view it is best to treat a quantifier like *nobody* as an operator which makes a sentence out of a one-place predicate. It would thus be of category (s/(s/n)). See how it goes: a one-place predicate is of category (s/n) because it makes an s (a sentence) out of an n (a name), and so an (s/(s/n)) makes a sentence out of something which makes a sentence out of a name. (This by itself doesn't solve all problems. The adventurous should look at why

(14) *nobody sees Bruce*

or

(15) *Julie sees nobody*

cannot be derived by these rules.)

Another kind of symbol is a one-place predicate modifier. Take the adverb *quickly* and look at

(16) *Adriane runs quickly*

The right way to treat this sentence is to suppose that **runs quickly** is a complex one-place predicate, i.e. a complex expression in category (s/n). Thus it would be that complex expression, **runs quickly**, which would make the sentence (16) out of the name **Adriane**. This shews incidentally how a categorial language could have complex expressions in other categories besides s. In that respect this extended language is unlike $\mathcal{L}$. But if **runs quickly** is to be in category (s/n) how does it get there? Well, **runs** is also in category (s/n), and surely the function of **quickly** is to form the complex predicate **runs quickly** out of the simpler predicate **runs**. **quickly** itself is therefore in category ((s/n)/(s/n)) since it makes an (s/n), a one-place predicate, out of an (s/n).

An even more elaborate category is that of preposition. Take the sentence

(17) **Bruce runs from David**

In (17) it seems reasonable to take

(18) **runs from David**

as a complex predicate - in category (s/n). So **from David** would be a predicate modifier in category ((s/n)/(s/n)). What does **from** do on its own then? Well it makes this modifier out of the name **David**, and so is in category (((s/n)/(s/n))/n). Sometimes it is more perspicuous to represent facts like this in a tree:

(19)

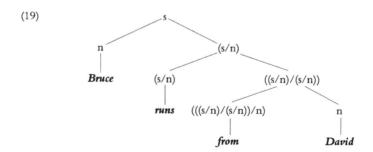

Example (19) could be elaborated by annotating the higher nodes with the complex expressions derived at each stage.

(20)

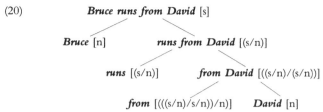

Bruce runs from David [s]

Bruce [n]   **runs from David** [(s/n)]

runs [(s/n)]   **from David** [((s/n)/(s/n))]

from [(((s/n)/s/n))/n)]   **David** [n]

The rules by which the next level up are obtained from the lower levels should be intuitively obvious. Thus the top s in (19) is obtained by the (s/n) applying to the n, and so on. But in order to state them precisely we need to give a formal definition of syntactic category. I shall use the letters σ and τ, sometimes with subscripts, as metalinguistic variables for syntactic categories. The set of syntactic categories is defined as follows:

> Syn1 s and n are syntactic categories
> Syn2 If σ and $\tau_1,...,\tau_k$ are all syntactic categories then so is
> $(\sigma/\tau_1...\tau_k)$

An expression in category $(\sigma/\tau_1...\tau_k)$ is often called a *functor*. It makes an expression in category σ out of k expressions in, respectively, categories $\tau_1,...,\tau_k$. These latter are sometimes called the *arguments* of the functor. This usage is because, when we come to interpret the functor semantically, its value will be a set-theoretical function whose arguments in the set-theoretical sense of 'argument' are the values of the expressions the functor applies to. In setting up $\mathscr{L}$, and the extensions described in (13)–(20), I have sometimes placed a functor between or after its arguments. On page 78 of Cresswell 1973 I explained why this makes no semantical difference. In using categorial languages for syntactical purposes a more elaborate notation is sometimes invoked to indicate where the functor is permitted to go. The concerns of this chapter do not demand that we go into these matters so what I shall do is, when I state the rules in a purely general form, assume that a functor always precedes its arguments, but when I deal with particular examples I shall put the functor in the place which most naturally corresponds with English.

All the formation rules can now be expressed completely generally. We can say that a sequence of symbols of $\mathscr{L}$ qualifies as an expression α of category σ in just one of the following two ways:

> FR4 If α is a symbol of category σ then α is an expression of
> category σ.

11

FR5   If δ is an expression of category $(\sigma/\tau_1...\tau_n)$ and $\alpha_1,...,\alpha_n$ are
expressions in, respectively, categories $\tau_1,...,\tau_n$, then the
sequence $(\delta\alpha_1...\alpha_n)$ is an expression in category σ.

Provided that each symbol is assigned a syntactic category then FR4 and
FR5 determine the class of well-formed expressions of the language. I
have said nothing about what symbols *are*. In considering a language
simply as a structure this doesn't matter, but if we are looking at a natural
language oughtn't we to say what symbols are? Many philosophers might
be tempted to say that symbols are *types* of which the *tokens* are sounds or
marks on paper. At this stage I don't want to say anything more about
that answer beyond saying that I find it more obscure than the problem.
When we speak, we do indeed, usually, make noises. When we write, we
do indeed mark paper, but whether we produce any *things* which could
be called tokens of symbols seems to me a highly contentious matter.
Splitting up the physical activity of language-using has to be an
idealization, so all I shall assume is that we have idealized to the point
that we can represent concrete pieces of language use as events which
have, at a certain level, an analysis in terms of linguistic expressions as
sequences of symbols.

For simplicity I shall assume that $\mathcal{L}$ is to be a disambiguated language.
For syntax this entails that no symbol is in more than one syntactic
category, nor is any symbol itself a complex expression. Some authors
relax these requirements but I am trying to keep everything as simple as I
can so that we can get to the issues that I want to discuss. So much then
for syntax. Let us go back to the language $\mathcal{L}$ defined by FR1-FR3. Our
aim is to shew how to interpret this language.

In Cresswell 1978 I claimed that to know what a sentence means is to
know the difference between a world in which the sentence is true and
one in which it is false. And, as stated there, this leads directly to possible-
worlds semantics. There are, to be sure, ontological questions about the
nature of possible worlds. What I shall do now though is set out a
possible-worlds semantics for $\mathcal{L}$ so that we may consider these questions
later in so far as they apply to semantics. So we begin with a set W of
possible worlds. But $\mathcal{L}$ doesn't only talk about worlds, it also talks about
things. After all we have names like ***Adriane***, ***Bruce***, ***Julie*** and ***David***, and
so our universe of discourse, the things we want to talk about, must
contain Adriane, Bruce, Julie and David - at least if those names apply to
the people we suppose them to apply to. So assume that D is the domain

or universe of things. By 'things' I mean to include anything we may want to talk about. Metaphysicians may wish to set limits on what that might be – some might eschew all but particular concrete physical objects. As far as semantics is concerned we set no limits in advance. I return to this issue on page 43.

Symbols of $\mathscr{L}$ have semantic values. Further, a crucial feature of language is its *conventionality*. What this means is that the semantic value of a symbol – its meaning if you like – is not part of the intrinsic nature of the symbol. This is not an accident. The whole point of language is to be able to talk about things when they are not present, and where we cannot rely on any *natural* connection to lead us from linguistic expressions to things. But the conventionality is constrained. It is true that the individual words of our language have the meaning that they do by convention, but it is part of that very same convention to determine the meanings of the complex items, in particular the meanings of sentences. This feature of language is known as its *compositionality*. Sometimes the principle of compositionality is known as *Frege's Principle*, and its exact formulation is a matter of some controversy. For now all I shall do is shew how it applies to $\mathscr{L}$.

In order to see what meanings *are* I shall follow the suggestion in Lewis 1972 and consider what meanings do. The meanings of names are, as far as $\mathscr{L}$ goes, just members of D. Suppose that Adriane and Bruce are in D. (D, recall, is a class of things. Classes have members and the symbol for class membership is $\in$. If a is one of the things which is a member of D we write $a \in D$ to indicate this. There is a technical distinction in set theory between sets and classes. All sets are classes but not *vice versa*. This distinction does not concern us at present.)

Suppose then that the meaning of ***Adriane*** is Adriane, and that the meaning of ***Bruce*** is Bruce. What this amounts to is that we have a correlation in the form of a list:

(21)   ***Adriane*** Adriane
     Bruce   Bruce

But calling it a list is misleading. For that suggests that *both* ***Adriane*** and Adriane, and ***Bruce*** and Bruce, are names, i.e. linguistic items. And the point is that while ***Adriane*** is a name Adriane is a person. The apparent paradox may be easily resolved by making a distinction between language and metalanguage. For although the correlation *described* in (21) is a correlation between words and things, the description of this correlation is given in a language. Not the language $\mathscr{L}$ that we are studying but the, basically English though enriched with symbols, language in which this book is being written. Example (21) is not the only correlation. Look at

(22)   ***Adriane*** Bruce
     Bruce   Adriane

Now (22) is not as plausible as (21) as a representation of English since ***Adriane*** is a woman's name and ***Bruce*** is a man's name, and Adriane is a woman while Bruce is a man. Yet if we think of a correlation as no more than a class of pairings (22) is just as much a correlation as (21) is.

It might be thought that (21) has a claim to being the 'right' correlation for another reason, that in (21) there is a natural connection between ***Adriane*** and Adriane – they are spelled the same. But this would be a mistake. It is simply an accident of the metalanguage in which (21) is stated. For although the name ***Adriane*** may have a spelling, Adriane herself is not a name and does not have a spelling. And even ***Adriane*** as a symbol of $\mathscr{L}$ need not have a spelling. For the boldface italic writing of that name is merely the way that the metalanguage in which this book is written picks out a symbol of $\mathscr{L}$. I have gone through this in some detail since I believe that a lot of confusion has resulted in semantics from not keeping the distinction clear.

I have spoken of a correlation or of a list. It is time to be more precise. The word 'list' is misleading in its suggestion of something which is written down. 'Correlation' is better because (21) is no more than a class of pairs. When ***Adriane*** is the first term in a pair in this correlation then Adriane is the second term, and when ***Bruce*** is the first term Bruce is the second. The pairs in this class are what are called *ordered pairs* because the order is important. Time for some more set-theoretical notation. If a and b are two things then we use:

(23) $\{a,b\}$

to refer to the class whose members are just a and b. (a and b have to be things which are eligible to be members of classes. For technical reasons some things are 'too big' for this to happen.) Thus we have that a and b are members of (23):

(24) $a \in \{a,b\}$, $b \in \{a,b\}$

Further only a and b are, i.e. for any c:

(25) If $c \in \{a,b\}$ then $c = a$ or $c = b$.

14

Since $\{a,b\}$ is no more than the class whose members are a and b, there is no question of the *order* of these elements

(26) $\{a,b\} = \{b,a\}$

The notation of (23) can be generalized since we frequently want to speak of classes with more than two members. So we use

(27) $\{a_1,\ldots,a_n\}$

to indicate the class whose members are precisely $a_1,\ldots,a_n$. Where a class is infinite we cannot refer to it by listing, but we can sometimes refer to it by description. Take the class of all even numbers. Sometimes you find people saying things like

(28) {2,4,6,...,etc.}

but that is somewhat vague because of the 'etc.'. A better way is to say

(29) {n:n is even}

Example (29) can be read as 'the class of all n such that n is even', and the general principle which defines it is

(30) m ∈ {n:n is even} iff m is even

Put more generally, where x and y refer to entities of any kind and Fx is a sentence about x then

(31) $y \in \{x{:}Fx\}$ iff Fy

y is in the class of x's such that Fx iff Fy. Example (31) can also be written as

(32) $x \in \{x{:}Fx\}$ iff Fx

provided we realize that the occurrences of the x *outside* the class description $\{x{:}Fx\}$ can be replaced by any other symbol which refers to things of the appropriate kind without the replacement having to be made inside the class description. (Those of you familiar with the predicate calculus can think of the x in $\{x{:}Fx\}$ as a bound variable. Thus $\{x{:}Fx\} = \{y{:}Fy\} = \{z{:}Fz\}$ and so on.)

In contrast to $\{a,b\}$ which might be thought of as an *unordered* pair we frequently want to speak of an *ordered pair*. We use the notation $\langle a,b\rangle$ to refer to the pair consisting of a and b in that order. It is tempting to speak of a as the first member of $\langle a,b\rangle$ and of b as its second member. This is harmless although technically a and b are not strictly members in the set-theoretical sense of $\langle a,b \rangle$. It is more correct to speak of a as the first *term* of $\langle a,b \rangle$ and of b as its second term.

With this notation we may refer to (21) as

(33) $\langle \textbf{\textit{Adriane}}, \text{Adriane} \rangle$
        $\langle \textbf{\textit{Bruce}}, \text{Bruce} \rangle$

and (22) as

(34) $\langle \textbf{\textit{Adriane}}, \text{Bruce} \rangle$
        $\langle \textbf{\textit{Bruce}}, \text{Adriane} \rangle$

If **Adriane** and **Bruce** were the only names in $\mathscr{L}$ then the meaning assignment to the names of $\mathscr{L}$ according to (21) would be

(35) $\{\langle \textbf{\textit{Adriane}}, \text{Adriane} \rangle, \langle \textbf{\textit{Bruce}}, \text{Bruce} \rangle\}$

and the meaning assignment according to (22) would be

(36) $\{\langle \textbf{\textit{Adriane}}, \text{Bruce} \rangle, \langle \textbf{\textit{Bruce}}, \text{Adriane} \rangle\}$

Thinking of correlations as sets of pairs allows infinite as well as finite correlations and allows much bigger meaning assignments than (35) or (36).

I said earlier that $\mathscr{L}$ is to be a disambiguated language. In the case of names this has to be an idealization, since there are many people named **Adriane** and many more named **Bruce**. The usual response is to say that in $\mathscr{L}$ there are a family of distinct names each of which names one person. All members of this family have a single surface realization. So as far as $\mathscr{L}$ is concerned the correlations are *functions*. This is the set-theoretical sense of function and should not be confused with the ordinary sense of the function of an artifact or organism. This latter sense of function is often used in discussions of functionalism in the philosophy of mind. In the set-theoretical sense what makes something a function is that the same first term is correlated with just one second term. So (33) and (34) are functions but

(37) $\{\langle \textbf{\textit{Adriane}}, \text{Adriane} \rangle, \langle \textbf{\textit{Adriane}}, \text{Bruce} \rangle\}$

is not. Put more generally, a class A of ordered pairs is a *function* provided that

(38) If $\langle a,b \rangle \in A$ and $\langle a,c \rangle \in A$, then $b = c$.

If A *is* a function then any a which is the first term of an ordered pair in A is said to be in the *domain* of A. Thus the domain of (33) is $\{$**Adriane**,

Bruce}. For *a* in the domain of A we often use the notation A(*a*) to indicate the (unique) *b* such that

(39) ⟨*a*,*b*⟩ ∈ A

In such a case we say that the function A has the value *b* for the argument *a*. You can think of functions in a dynamic way by thinking of *a* as the input and *b* as the output. If A is a list of pairs then when *a* is the input you find the pair whose first term is *a*. The second term of that pair will be the output. Of course this depends on the requirement that for any given *a* there is at most one *b* such that ⟨*a*,*b*⟩ ∈ A. The dynamic metaphor is no more than that. Each person has at most one mother so if A is the function 'mother of' we can correlate each *a* with the unique *b* who is *a*'s mother. (Notice that many people can have the same mother. A function is a many-to-one relation. All that is required is that no person have more than one mother.) It is obviously metaphorical to think of a person as an input and their mother as an output. This is why the account of a function as a set of ordered pairs is more accurate and less misleading.

We can illustrate this using (33) and (34) since these are functions. Call (33) V_1 and (34) V_2. Then we have the following

(40) V_1(***Adriane***) = Adriane
(41) V_1(***Bruce***) = Bruce

This is because Adriane is the unique *b* such that

(42) ⟨***Adriane***,*b*⟩ ∈ V_1

and Bruce is the unique *b* such that

(43) ⟨***Bruce***,*b*⟩ ∈ V_1

Similarly

(44) V_2(***Adriane***) = Bruce
(45) V_2(***Bruce***) = Adriane

V_1 and V_2 represent two distinct meaning assignments to $\mathscr{L}$. We can now for the first time state a particular instance of the question to be investigated in this book. Which one of these assignments is the right one?

It is important at this stage to distinguish the question that we are interested in from a question that we are not. In specifying the semantic interpretation for a language like $\mathscr{L}$ we are going to add to our stock of the set W of possible worlds and the set D of 'things' a function which we shall call V which assigns to every symbol α of $\mathscr{L}$ an entity $V(\alpha)$ which is the meaning of α according to V. An *interpretation* for $\mathscr{L}$ will then be an ordered triple $\langle W,D,V \rangle$ whose first term is a set of possible worlds, whose second term is a domain of things and whose third term is an assignment function whose nature is shortly to be specified. (An ordered triple is the obvious generalization of an ordered pair. Even more generally for any given $a_1,...,a_n$ there is the (ordered) n-tuple, $\langle a_1,...,a_n \rangle$ consisting of a_1 to a_n in that order.) Now it is tempting to put the question, for a given interpretation, of just *why* W, D and V are the way they are. In one sense this is a non-question. Look at V_1 and V_2. Suppose I ask: Why is $V_1(\textbf{\textit{Adriane}})$, Adriane? If the question is why I called the list in (33) V_1, and the list in (34) V_2, then the answer is that I had two functions that I wanted to talk to you about and therefore I needed two metalinguistic names for them. If you ask why are those functions what they are, the only reply is that among the many sets of pairs there are the ones I am calling V_1 and V_2, and they are what they are because that's what they are.

You may wonder why I am labouring the obvious fact that this is a non-question. Well, it turns out that certain views about the reduction of semantic terms to non-semantic terms consist in claiming that there is no question to answer. For suppose someone is worried about why it is that in English *Adriane* refers to Adriane. We say that the semantics of English is given by V_1 and so the question of why *Adriane* refers to Adriane is just the question of why $V_1(\textbf{\textit{Adriane}})$ = Adriane, and we have seen that that is a non-question. (At this point I ought to mention that regarding the meaning of names as simply the things they denote is a controversial issue in philosophy. It would for instance make the sentence

(46) *Adriane is Allison*

provided *is* is identity, a necessary truth. Yet surely you need more than logical acumen to know that (46) is true. These problems won't affect present issues.) Part of the problem is how to define 'English'. If we use V_1 as part of the *definition* of English then there is no non-trivial answer to the question of why, in English, *Adriane* refers to Adriane. In fact the only non-trivial question is whether English speakers use the words *Adriane* and *Bruce* in such a way that V_1 is a correct model or V_2 is. But then we face the question: what is it about speakers of a language which makes it the case that they are using *Adriane* and *Bruce* in the V_1 way, or using them in the V_2 way? This isn't a question of how we know. It is a question of what is being claimed when we claim they use words one way rather than another way. This is the question that later chapters will be addressing. But the problem of course does not arise only in the case of names. It affects the symbols of every category. For that reason the next chapter will explain how the meanings of other expressions in a given interpretation are determined.

2

Predicates and functors

Meanings of whole sentences of $\mathscr{L}$ are sets of worlds. Actually this isn't quite right since a sentence like (6) on page 6 could be true at one time and false at another. We must pretend that all the sentences of our restricted little language $\mathscr{L}$ are understood as referring to some particular time. But whole sentences are complex expressions, and according to Frege's Principle, their meanings depend on the meanings of the symbols in them, together with the rules for combining those meanings. It is here that the categorial description of the syntax of $\mathscr{L}$ becomes relevant. Consider the one-place predicates of $\mathscr{L}$. They are **runs** and **whistles**. In a categorial description one-place predicates turn a name into a sentence. Now among the set of all possible worlds there will be those in which (at the particular time that we are assuming $\mathscr{L}$ to be talking about) Adriane is running. Call this set p. There will also be the set of worlds in which Bruce is running. Call this set q. At this point we have to remember that worlds, whatever they are, are not linguistic things. That Adriane is running in a world, or that Bruce is running in a world, is something which in some sense is 'out there' and which can be referred to in $\mathscr{L}$. So it will be a constraint on that V which gets closest to English that

(1)   V(**Adriane runs**) = p

and

(2)   V(**Bruce runs**) = q.

In this last sentence V is being used as a metalogical variable, for there are many functions in the sense of many correlations between expressions of $\mathscr{L}$ and things which can be their meanings. So what would the meaning of **runs** be? If you think about it you will see that part at least of what the meaning of **runs** does is get you from Adriane to p, and from Bruce to q. So that part of its meaning may be captured by

(3) ⟨Adriane, *p*⟩
     ⟨Bruce, *q*⟩

Why did we make it (3) rather than

(4) ⟨***Adriane***, *p*⟩
     ⟨***Bruce***, *q*⟩ ?

That is, why did we associate the set of worlds in which Adriane runs with Adriane rather than with her name? Well (3) may be thought of as a recipe for getting us from each of Adriane and Bruce to the set of worlds in which that person runs. This can be thought of as a language-independent set-theoretical entity which can be the meaning of ***runs***. Example (4) will certainly give us the same result as (3) if we are in a language in which the meanings of ***Adriane*** and ***Bruce*** are given by V_1, but it will give the wrong result if they are given by V_2, for in the latter case ***Adriane*** refers to Bruce, but *p* is not the set of worlds in which Bruce runs, but the set of worlds in which Adriane runs. So if we want the meaning of ***runs*** to be something which is not dependent on the meaning of other words in $\mathscr{L}$ then we must make it like (3) rather than (4).

   If we try to generalize (3) we say that it is a set of ordered pairs, the first term of which is a member of D, and the second term of which is a set of possible worlds. A set of possible worlds is just a subset of W and we can write

(5) $p \subseteq W$
(6) $q \subseteq W$

to indicate that both *p* and *q* are subsets of W. Do not confuse $\subseteq$ with $\in$. To say that $p \subseteq W$ is not to say that *p* is a member of W; it is to say that any world which is a member of *p* is also a member of W. The members of W are worlds, thus $w_1 \in W$, $w_2 \in W$, and so on. The subsets of W are sets of worlds. Put more generally, if Γ and Δ are any classes then we say that

(7) $\Gamma \subseteq \Delta$

iff

(8) For every *a* such that $a \in \Gamma$, $a \in \Delta$.

For those familiar with predicate-calculus notation we have

(9) $\Gamma \subseteq \Delta$ iff $\forall x(x \in \Gamma \supset x \in \Delta)$.

If we generalize (3) then the meaning of a one-place predicate is a function whose domain is taken from D and whose values are all subsets of W. Supposing ω is such a function. The symbol 'ω' here is part of the enriched English metalanguage we are using, and refers to a function. The function itself is not a linguistic entity. For example ω might be just (3). In this case its domain is simply Adriane and Bruce (the people, not their names) and its range, i.e. the things that can be its values, will be the sets p and q. Using set-theoretical terminology this means that

(10) ω(Adriane) = p
(11) ω(Bruce) = q

Of course if ω is really to represent running, its domain will contain many more people than Adriane and Bruce.

We now have functions of two different kinds, and it is important not to confuse them. We have earlier spoken of an assignment function V to $\mathscr{L}$. V is a function whose arguments are linguistic expressions and whose values are the kind of things which are their meanings. But in the case of some expressions, for instance one-place predicates as we have just seen, these meanings are themselves functions. Thus we might have, for some meaning assignment V

(12) V(*runs*) = ω

This means that, if ω is (3), then V is a function whose value for the argument *runs*, where *runs* is a one-place predicate, is the function ω. ω then appears as the value of one function, V, for an argument, *runs*; but it is also itself a function whose value for the argument Adriane (not, remember, *Adriane*) is p, and whose value for Bruce is q.

We now have the apparatus to specify the values of atomic sentences consisting of a name and a one-place predicate. It should be obvious now how to deal with the sentence

(13) *Adriane runs*

The rule is quite simple:

(14) V(*Adriane runs*) = V(*runs*)(V(*Adriane*))

V(*runs*) we suppose is ω and V(*Adriane*) is Adriane. So V(*runs*)(V(*Adriane*)) is simply

(15) ω(Adriane)

and this we recall is *p*, the set of worlds in which Adriane runs. The principle used for (13) applies to all sentences made up in accordance with FR1.

(16) $V(aF) = V(F)(V(a))$

That is, the value of *aF* according to V will be the result of taking the function which is the value of *F*, and this we know is itself a function from D to subsets of W, and applying that function to the member of D which is the value according to V of the name *a*.

Notice that (16) is a rule which applies to every interpretation. Sometimes, as for instance in (14), I am talking about the particular V which is intended to represent English. The letter 'V' is a metalinguistic symbol which sometimes names the 'intended' interpretation, but in other cases, like (16), counts as a variable intended to describe a feature shared by every interpretation to $\mathscr{L}$. The distinction is important since the question this book is concerned with is just the question of what it is about speakers of a language that makes one particular $\langle$W,D,V$\rangle$ the right interpretation for the language they speak rather than another one. And this question cannot be answered without *first* saying what a $\langle$W,D,V$\rangle$ has to be in order to count as an interpretation for $\mathscr{L}$, whether it be the correct one or an incorrect one.

FR2 is the obvious extension of FR1. A two-place predicate makes a sentence out of two names. Since the order of the names is important the meaning of such a predicate will need to be a set of triples. If D contains only Adriane and Bruce then the meaning of a two-place predicate like **sees** will be a function from ordered pairs of these two arguments to sets of worlds. By analogy with running we may suppose that seeing is a relation between two members of D. (Actually we know that seeing is more complicated than that – we see people doing things – but for now I'll pretend that all we see is members of D, and for now that just means Adriane and Bruce.) So let *p*, *q*, *r* and *s* be respectively the set of worlds in which (*p*) Adriane sees Adriane, (*q*) Bruce sees Bruce, (*r*) Adriane sees Bruce and (*s*) Bruce sees Adriane. Then V(**sees**) might be

(17) $\langle$Adriane, Adriane, *p*$\rangle$
      $\langle$Bruce, Bruce, *q*$\rangle$
      $\langle$Adriane, Bruce, *r*$\rangle$
      $\langle$Bruce, Adriane, *s*$\rangle$

Again using 'ω' as a metalinguistic variable we may refer to (17) as ω. The rule for evaluating say

(18) **Bruce sees Adriane**

will be

(19) V(*sees*)(V(**Bruce**), V(**Adriane**))

that is,

ω(Bruce, Adriane)

and given that ω is (17) then (20) is *s*, the set of worlds in which Bruce sees Adriane. The rule for sentences in accordance with FR2 in *any* interpretation ⟨W,D,V⟩ is just

(20) V(*aFb*) = V(*F*)(V(*a*),V(*b*))

We have now shewn how values are determined for all the atomic sentences given that we have values for all the simple symbols. The complex sentences are those obtained from the simple ones in accordance with FR3. There are two ways we can proceed at this point. The sentential functors of $\mathscr{L}$ are all what are often called logical constants, and if we were to follow the standard practice in logic we would say something like this:

(21) α *not* is true if α is false and false if α is true.
(22) (α *and* β) is true if α and β are both true, otherwise it is false.
(23) (*if* αβ) is true if α is false or β is true. It is false only if α is true and β is false.

Example (23) reflects the meaning of 'if' usually called *material implication* and symbolized in logic by ⊃ or by →. It is a controversial question whether *if* in English and the corresponding words of other languages really do have this meaning.

Examples (21)-(23) have been formulated using simply the notion of truth. But $\mathscr{L}$ has a possible–worlds semantics and so its sentences are true in some worlds and false in others. For any interpretation ⟨W,D,V⟩, and any sentence α, V(α) is a set of worlds, the worlds in which, according to V, α is true. This means that (21) should be rewritten to say for any world *w*:

(24) α *not* is true in *w* iff α is false in *w*. Otherwise α *not* is false in *w*.

Put in set-theoretical notation (24) is

(25) $w \in V(\alpha \; \textbf{not})$ iff $w \notin V(\alpha)$

I hope you can see that (25) is just (24) in symbolic notation with the reference to V made explicit. For **and** and **if** we have:

(26) $w \in V(\alpha \; \textbf{and} \; \beta)$ iff $w \in \alpha$ and $w \in \beta$
(27) $w \in V(\textbf{if} \; \alpha\beta)$ iff either $w \notin V(\alpha)$ or $w \in V(\beta)$

This way of proceeding, however, makes the role of **not**, **and** and **if** rather special. Because when you look at (25)–(27) you will see that, unlike the case of predicates, V does not assign to **not**, **and** and **if** set-theoretical entities which can count as their meanings. When we do logic this does not matter since the symbols which correspond to those words are regarded as constants with a fixed meaning in all interpretations. But when we want to study the structure of a natural language its conventionality requires that we consider interpretations in which **not**, **and** and **if** need not have the meanings given to them by (21)–(27).

Look first at the case of **not**. In a categorial language its syntactic category is (s/s). It makes a sentence out of a sentence. Since the meaning of a sentence in a particular interpretation for $\mathscr{L}$ is a set of worlds then the meaning of **not** will need to be a function which, when offered as argument the set of worlds in which α is true, delivers the set of worlds in which α **not** is true. Let ω be this function. Then

(28) $V(\alpha \; \textbf{not}) = \omega(V(\alpha))$

In fact we can equally express this as

(29) $V(\alpha \; \textbf{not}) = V(\textbf{not})(V(\alpha))$

Example (29) tells us how to get the meaning of α **not** from the meanings of **not** and α. It does not of itself tell us what the meaning of **not** is. We know that $V(\textbf{not})$ has to be a function whose arguments are sets of worlds and whose values are sets of worlds. As a set of ordered pairs this means that all its members will have the form $\langle p,q \rangle$ where $p \subseteq W$ and $q \subseteq W$. If $V(\textbf{not})$ reflects (25) it will be the function ω such that if $p \subseteq W$, and $w \in W$:

(30) $w \in \omega(p)$ iff $w \notin p$

In (30) we have specified which set of worlds $\omega(p)$ is by saying whether or not any particular $w \in W$ is in it or not. Using the set-theoretical notion of complement, where $W - p$ is just those members of W not in p we have as equivalent to (30):

(31) $\omega(p) = W - p$

See how to put (29) and (30) together to get (25):

(32) $w \in V(\alpha \ \boldsymbol{not})$ iff $w \in V(\boldsymbol{not})(V(\alpha))$ (by (29)), iff $w \notin V(\alpha)$ (by (30) with $V(\alpha)$ as the set p, and $V(\boldsymbol{not})$ as ω)

What (29) and (30) do is to divide the labour of getting to the meaning of (25) into the part that gives the meaning of the particular symbol *not* and the part that shews how the meaning of a sentence obtained using a one-place sentential functor is got from the meaning of its parts. Example (29) could stand even if (31) is changed to reflect a language in which *not* meant 'it is so that'. When we speak of one-place functors using metalinguistic variables we usually put the functor in front of its arguments, and so where δ is *any* one-place functor we have

(33) $V(\delta\alpha) = V(\delta)(V(\alpha))$

We can now proceed more quickly with *and* and *if*. The general rule for a two-place functor δ is of course

(34) $V(\delta\alpha\beta) = V(\delta)(V(\alpha),V(\beta))$

To get (26) we assume that $V(\boldsymbol{and})$ is the function such that where p and q are sets of worlds and w is a world:

(35) $w \in V(\boldsymbol{and})(p,q)$ iff $w \in p$ and $w \in q$

Where $\cap$ is the set-theoretical operation forming the set whose members are common to p and q we may express (35) as

(36) $V(\boldsymbol{and})(p,q) = p \cap q$

By (34) and (35) we have

(37) $w \in V(\alpha \ \boldsymbol{and} \ \beta)$ iff $w \in V(\boldsymbol{and})(V(\alpha),V(\beta))$
      iff $w \in V(\alpha)$ and $w \in V(\beta)$, which is (26).
(38) $w \in V(\boldsymbol{if})(p,q)$ iff $w \notin p$ or $w \in q$

I trust it is clear how to get (27) from (38) and (34).

The structural principles (16), (20), (33) and (34) can all be stated using the rules FR4 and FR5 in a categorial language. For FR4 we know already that if α is a name then $V(\alpha) \in D$. If there were any simple sentence symbols they would be assigned subsets of W. Where α is a symbol in a functor category, say $(\sigma/\tau_1...\tau_n)$ then $V(\alpha)$ will be a function from the kinds of things which are the values of expressions in categories $\tau_1,...,\tau_n$ respectively, to the kinds of things which are the values of expressions in category σ. Thus **runs** is in category (s/n) so its value has to be a function from things which are the values of names - i.e. members of D - to things which are the values of sentences, subsets of W. **and** is in category (s/ss) so its value will be a function which takes pairs of subsets of W, to a subset of W. If we had a predicate modifier in category $((s/n)/(s/n))$ *its* value would be a function which takes the value of a predicate in (s/n), i.e. takes a function from D to subsets at W to another such function, and so on.

Where δ is in category $(\sigma/\tau_1...\tau_n)$ and $\alpha_1,...,\alpha_n$ are, respectively, in categories $\tau_1,...,\tau_n$, then the value of the expression $(\delta\alpha_1...\alpha_n)$, formed in accordance with FR5, is specified by:

(39) $\quad V(\delta\alpha_1...\alpha_n) = V(\delta)(V(\alpha_1),...,V(\alpha_n))$

To complete the description of $\mathscr{L}$ I shall add one more one-place sentential operator - the word **possibly**. This goes in front of its argument so that if α is a sentence of $\mathscr{L}$ so is **possibly** α. Example (33) still applies but we need to specify the meaning of **possibly** in the intended interpretation. The reason for introducing **possibly** is that so far the possible worlds have not played any essential role in the semantics. For whether $w \in V(\textbf{runs})(a)$ depends only on whether or not a runs in w, and the values of sentences made up by **not**, **and** and **if** in a world depend only on the values of their arguments in that world. **possibly** is different. There are of course different senses of 'possible'. The logically possible is what is true in at least one world. So it is logically possible that I should fly to the moon without wearing a space suit. A more realistic sense of 'possible' would not allow this. (See Kratzer 1977.) But even if we restrict ourselves to a precise sense of possible, what is possible depends on what the world is like. If I break my leg it will no longer be possible that I run. So let us fix on some particular sense of possibility and suppose that from each possible world certain other worlds are possible. Write w_1Rw_2 to mean that w_2 is a possible world relative to w_1. Given such a notion of possibility then we want to say that **possibly** α is true in w_1 iff α is itself true in w_2 for some w_2 such that w_1Rw_2. To get this meaning we must make $V(\textbf{possibly})$ the function such that for any world w_1 and any $p \subseteq W$,

(40) $\quad w_1 \in V(\textbf{possibly})(p)$ iff there exists $w_2 \in W$ such that w_1Rw_2 and $w_2 \in p$.

As a test of all this I shall go through a version of (7) on page 7 with **possibly** added, to shew what meaning it has in the intended interpretation.

(41) (*if Adriane runs not (Julie whistles and possibly Bruce sees David*))

The atomic sentences are (8), (9) and (10). I shall repeat them here:

> **Adriane runs**
> **Julie whistles**
> **Bruce sees David**

The meanings of these sentences in any interpretation $\langle W, D, V \rangle$ are, respectively,

(42) $V(runs)V(Adriane)$
(43) $V(whistles)V(Julie)$
(44) $V(sees)(V(Bruce), V(David))$

In the intended interpretation $V(runs)$ is the function ω_1 which takes $a \in D$ to the set of worlds in which a runs, $V(whistles)$ is the function ω_2 which takes any $a \in D$ to the set of worlds in which a whistles, and $V(sees)$ is the function ω_3 which takes any pair a and b into the set of worlds in which a sees b. With $V(Adriane) = $ Adriane, $V(Julie) = $ Julie, $V(Bruce) = $ Bruce, $V(David) = $ David then the semantics of (8), (9) and (10) on page 7 become, respectively,

(45) ω_1(Adriane)
(46) ω_2(Julie)
(47) ω_3(Bruce, David)

And these will be, respectively, the set of worlds, call it p, in which Adriane runs, the set of worlds, call it q, in which Julie whistles, and the set of worlds, call it r, in which Bruce sees David. The sentence

(48) **Possibly Bruce sees David**

will then have the meaning

(49) $V(possibly)(r)$

and $w_1 \in$ (49) iff there is some $w_2 \in W$ such that $w_1 R w_2$ and $w_2 \in r$. And this will mean that (48) is true in a world w_1 iff there is a world w_2 possible relative to w_1 in which Bruce sees David. Let us use s to mean the set of all such worlds. That is, any $w \in s$ iff w is a world in which it is possible that Bruce sees David, i.e. it is a world from which you can get by R to another (possibly the same) world in which Bruce does see David. We can now evaluate (41). It is

(50) $\text{V}(if)(\text{V}(not)(p), \text{V}(and)(p,s))$

Satisfy yourself that this is really so. Now take any world w. $w \in \text{V}(50)$ iff, by (38), either

(51) $w \notin \text{V}(not)(p)$

or

(52) $w \in \text{V}(and)(p,s)$

Example (51) will hold by (30), iff $w \in p$, and (52) will hold by (35) iff $w \in p$ and $w \in s$. So (50) will be true in w iff either Adriane does run or Julie whistles and it is possible that Bruce sees David. Given that *if* is being interpreted as material implication this is the correct result, because given that Adriane does run the antecedent of (41), i.e.

(53) **Adriane runs not**

is false, and in that case we are not committed to the truth of the consequent. But if Adriane doesn't run (53) is true, and then for (41) to be true the consequent

(54) (**Julie whistles and possibly Bruce sees David**)

must be true too.

This finishes the description of $\mathscr{L}$ and its interpretations. It has been long but will enable us to raise the philosophical issues. The first comment is that $\mathscr{L}$ is what is sometimes called an intensional language. Look at $\text{V}(runs)$. $\text{V}(runs)$ is the function such that for any $a \in \text{D}$ in its domain $\text{V}(runs)(a)$ is the set of worlds in which a is running. At least that is so in what I am speaking of as the *intended* interpretation for $\mathscr{L}$. Given a world w we can form the set

(55) $\{a \in \text{D}: w \in \text{V}(runs)(a)\}$

This is the set consisting of all and only those a in D which have the property that $w \in \text{V}(runs)(a)$. Now $w \in \text{V}(runs)(a)$ iff a runs in w. So (55) is the set of those who run in w. This set is sometimes called the *extension* of $\text{V}(runs)$ in w. The extension of *runs* is not its meaning. Knowing who satisfies *runs* is neither necessary nor sufficient for knowing what *runs* means. What you need to know is what counts as running in each possible world. This is called the *intension* of *runs* and is another way of

Language in the world

expressing the meaning. Intension together with the world determines extension. I shall have more to say about this when we look at Putnam 1975.

I have spoken about the intended interpretation of $\mathscr{L}$, and it is now time to say something about what this means. In discussing the semantics of names on pages 17f., I have already begun to address this problem. What we have in $\mathscr{L}$ are a number of symbols that are displayed as if they were English words. These are then correlated with non-linguistic items, members of D, functions from these to sets of worlds and so on. In describing the semantics of $\mathscr{L}$ I have been doing two different things and it is important to stress the difference. First I have defined what counts as an interpretation for $\mathscr{L}$. An interpretation for $\mathscr{L}$ is *any* $\langle W,D,V \rangle$ triple in which W and D are sets and V is a function which assigns appropriate values to the symbols which then generate values for all the linguistic expressions in accordance with (39). This includes all the non-intended interpretations like the one mentioned in (35) on page 16. The second thing I have been doing is to specify what counts as the 'intended' interpretation for English. But what do we mean by the intended interpretation? Well it is presumably the one closest to English. And this gets us back to the question: what is English? One way is to answer it by *stipulation*. 'English' is a language in which **Adriane** means Adriane, **Bruce** means Bruce, **runs** means running and so on. I am not bothered about questions like what running is; I assume that there is a function that takes each individual into the set of worlds in which that individual runs and that in some sense that's what running *is* independently of how any language refers to it. Suppose that we do define that fragment of English that $\mathscr{L}$ represents as the pair consisting of $\mathscr{L}$ together with the $\langle W,D,V \rangle$ which is stipulated as the intended interpretation. Then if we ask the question *why* does **runs** in English mean running the answer is, as I mentioned earlier when talking about names, that this is a non-question. It means running because V in the $\langle W,D,V \rangle$ which constitutes English is such that V(**runs**) is the function ω which takes any $a \in D$ into the set of worlds $\omega(a)$ in which a runs. I believe that those who use Tarski's theory of truth as a way of defining semantic notions in terms of non-semantic notions are simply asking this non-question and I shall have more to say on this when I discuss Field's article on Tarski on pages 111–14.

If this question is a non-question, is there a question which is a real one? Let's go back to the ability defended in Cresswell 1978 as a speaker's semantic competence. What is it that a speaker knows who knows that

30

(56) **Adriane runs** is true in a world w iff Adriane runs in w?

It can hardly be that

(57) $w \in V(\textbf{Adriane runs})$ iff Adriane runs in w

since that fact is just the logically necessary fact that V is the function that it is. (You might want to follow Kripke 1972a and say that this is a necessary *a posteriori* truth, but in my view all such cases involve a contingent proposition somewhere. I shall have something to say about this issue when I discuss Putnam 1975.) Presumably what you know is that English speakers use

(58) **Adriane runs**

in a way which satisfies (56), or that a particular speaker on a particular occasion is so using it. So what we are interested in is what it is about a population that constitutes their speaking English. Of course 'English' could be defined as the language spoken by a certain population, and then (56) would be contingent. But either way the contingent question seems to be this: we have a linguistic community and they are using a language whose syntax can be described by $\mathscr{L}$. Among the possible interpretations there is one in which the symbols of $\mathscr{L}$ are correlated with the entities which are meanings in a way which gives them the truth conditions they have in the sentences as used. In Cresswell 1978 I argued that the fact that speakers were using language in such a way was an empirical phenomenon. What is important to realize is that nothing said so far in the description of $\mathscr{L}$ and its semantics gives us any indication whatever about what it is that constitutes a particular $\langle W,D,V \rangle$ as being the right one. The burden of Cresswell 1978 was to argue that even though we may have no analysis of what constitutes an interpretation's being correct yet we can and do know that, for instance, (56) holds. That is to say we know that English speakers do use (58) in a way which satisfies (56) even if we have no account to offer for what it is they are doing.

We shall be looking a little later at some answers which have been given to this question. One answer makes it depend on first having an account of beliefs, intentions and the like. This is what Stalnaker (1984) calls the pragmatic picture. If we adopt the pragmatic picture then we cannot analyse attitudes like belief in terms of language use, and so we shall look at Field's 1978 attempt to do just that and Stalnaker's criticism of it. Finally we shall look at arguments intended to shew that semantic facts are not reducible to non-semantic facts, even though they may logically supervene on them, and suggest why, if that is so, we can nevertheless know them. What I have tried to present so far is a simple formal language that we shall be able to come back to from time to time and use to help us understand the points that these various authors are making.

APPENDIX: SYNTAX AND SEMANTICS OF $\mathscr{L}$

(a) The set *Syn* of syntactic categories is the least set such that

    1 s $\in$ *Syn* and n $\in$ *Syn*
    2 if σ, and $\tau_1,...,\tau_n \in$ *Syn* then $(\sigma/\tau_1...\tau_n) \in$ *Syn*

(b) $\mathscr{L}$ contains symbols in categories n, (s/n), (s/nn), (s/s) and (s/ss):

    1 **Adriane**, **Bruce**, **Julie** and **David** are in category n
    2 **runs** and **whistles** are in category (s/n)
    3 **sees** is in category (s/nn)
    4 **not** and **possibly** are in category (s/s)
    5 **and** and **if** are in category (s/ss)

(c) If δ is in category $(\sigma/\tau_1...\tau_n)$ and $\alpha_1,...,\alpha_n$ are, respectively, in categories $\tau_1,..., \tau_n$, then $(\delta\alpha_1...\alpha_n)$ is a well-formed expression of $\mathscr{L}$ in category σ.

(Note: In the presentation of $\mathscr{L}$ on pages 5–7 the 'functor' (δ in (c)) sometimes is put between or after its 'arguments' ($\alpha_1,..., \alpha_n$). For comment on this see pages 6f., and 11.)

(d) An interpretation for $\mathscr{L}$ is a triple $\langle W,D,V \rangle$ in which W is a set of possible worlds, D a domain of 'things' and V a function such that where α is a symbol in category σ, $V(\alpha) \in D_\sigma$, where D_σ satisfies the following:

    1 $D_s = \mathscr{P}W$ ($\mathscr{P}W$ is the class of all subsets of W, i.e. $p \in \mathscr{P}W$ iff $p \subseteq W$)
    2 $D_n = D$
    3 $D_{(\sigma/\tau_1...\tau_n)}$ is a set of n-place functions (not necessarily total) whose arguments are taken from, respectively, $D_{\tau_1},...,D_{\tau_n}$, and whose values are in D_σ.

(e) Where $(\delta\alpha_1...\alpha_n)$ is a complex expression in category σ, then

$$V(\delta\alpha_1...\alpha_n) = V(\delta)(V(\alpha_1),...,V(\alpha_n))$$

3

The isomorphism problem

The last chapter raised the problem of deciding which interpretation is the correct one. I want now to raise a particular case of what is in fact the same problem. To do this I will take $\mathscr{L}$ and pretend that its intended interpretation is extremely small. I shall assume that W contains only two worlds w_1 and w_2 and that D contains only two individuals, say Adriane and Bruce, whom I shall refer to as a and b. I will assume that, for the interpretation of ***possibly***, w_1Rw_1, w_1Rw_2 and w_2Rw_2. That is, each world is possible relative to itself and w_2 is possible relative to w_1. Assume that a runs in w_1 and b runs in w_2, while a sees b in w_1 and b sees a in w_2. I shall ignore whistling. It is convenient to refer to running and seeing as ω_1 and ω_2, where

$$\omega_1 = \{\langle a,\{w_1\}\rangle, \langle b,\{w_2\}\rangle\}$$

What this means is that the set of worlds in which a runs is just $\{w_1\}$, i.e. the set whose only member is w_1, while the set of worlds in which b runs is $\{w_2\}$. To state ω_2 we need the symbol $\emptyset$, which stands for the empty set, the set which has no members. Then

$$\omega_2 = \{\langle a,a,\emptyset\rangle, \langle a,b,\{w_1\}\rangle, \langle b,a,\{w_2\}\rangle, \langle b,b,\emptyset\rangle\}$$

I shall assume that the sentential functors have the meanings given in (30), (35), (38) and (40) on pages 25–7. Assuming that the symbols of $\mathscr{L}$ (ignoring ***whistles***, ***Julie*** and ***David***) have the intended meanings, we may set out this interpretation, which I'll call $\langle W_1,D_1,V_1\rangle$, as follows:

$$
\begin{aligned}
W_1 &= \{w_1,w_2\} \\
D_1 &= \{a,b\} \\
V_1(\textbf{\textit{Adriane}}) &= a \\
V_1(\textbf{\textit{Bruce}}) &= b \\
V_1(\textbf{\textit{runs}}) &= \omega_1 \\
V_1(\textbf{\textit{sees}}) &= \omega_2
\end{aligned}
$$

The sentential functors receive their usual interpretation. It might help to use a picture

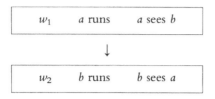

This, let us say, is the intended interpretation of $\mathscr{L}$. But now let us look at another interpretation, $\langle W_2, D_2, V_2 \rangle$. $\langle W_2, D_2, V_2 \rangle$ is to be what is called *isomorphic* to $\langle W_1, D_1, V_1 \rangle$. That means that it has exactly the same structure but is made up from different entities. Instead of the worlds w_1 and w_2 it has the numbers 1 and 2, and instead of a and b (Adriane and Bruce) it has the numbers 3 and 4. And instead of running and seeing it has the corresponding relations between numbers. Specifically, W_2 is simply the numbers 1 and 2 with R as $\leqslant$, while D_2 is the numbers 3 and 4. Let $\omega_1\star$ and $\omega_2\star$ be defined as follows:

$\omega_1\star = \{\langle 3, \{1\}\rangle, \langle 4, \{2\}\rangle\}$
$\omega_2\star = \{\langle 3,3,\emptyset\rangle, \langle 3,4,\{1\}\rangle, \langle 4,3,\{2\}\rangle, \langle 4,4,\emptyset\rangle\}$

We might describe $\omega_1\star$ by saying $\omega_1\star(3)$ is satisfied at the number 1 and at no other number, while $\omega_1\star(4)$ is satisfied at 2 and at no other number. Similarly $\omega_2\star(3,3)$ is never satisfied, $\omega_2\star(3,4)$ only at 1, $\omega_2\star(4,3)$ only at 2 and $\omega_2\star(4,4)$ never. If we write $\Omega_1(n)$ to mean that $\omega_1\star$ is satisfied and $\Omega_2(n,k)$ to mean that $\Omega_2\star(n,k)$ is satisfied ($n = 3,4$, $k = 3,4$), we may picture $\langle W_2, D_2, V_2 \rangle$ as

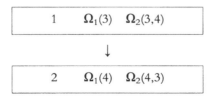

To complete the description of $\langle W_2, D_2, V_2 \rangle$ we have to say what V_2 is. It is

$V_2(\textbf{\textit{Adriane}})$ = 3
$V_2(\textbf{\textit{Bruce}})$ = 4
$V_2(\textbf{\textit{runs}})$ = $\omega_1\star$
$V_2(\textbf{\textit{sees}})$ = $\omega_2\star$

I hope you can see that $\langle W_1, D_1, V_1 \rangle$ and $\langle W_2, D_2, V_2 \rangle$ are quite different interpretations. Further I hope it is clear that $\langle W_1, D_1, V_1 \rangle$ is the intended one while $\langle W_2, D_2, V_2 \rangle$ is not. For if we are intending to model English **Adriane** refers to Adriane and not to the number 3, while **runs** refers to running and not to the number-theoretic function $\omega_1\star$. But $\langle W_1, D_1, V_1 \rangle$ and $\langle W_2, D_2, V_2 \rangle$ are isomorphic in the sense that anything said in the one exactly corresponds with everything said in the other. We must of course re-interpret the sentential functors so that for n = 1,2 and $p,q \subseteq \{1,2\}$, n $\in$ V(**not**)(p) iff n $\notin$ p, n $\in$ V(**and**)(p,q) iff n $\in$ p and n $\in$ q, and n $\in$ V(**if**)(p,q) iff n $\notin$ p or n $\in$ q, n $\in$ V(**possibly**)(p) iff m $\in$ p for some m $\leqslant$ n. Given all this it is easy to see that every sentence α of $\mathscr{L}$, whether simple or complex, has the property that

$w_1 \in V_1(\alpha)$ iff $1 \in V_2(\alpha)$
$w_2 \in V_1(\alpha)$ iff $2 \in V_2(\alpha)$

Suppose then w_1 is the actual world. (There is controversy about the metaphysics of that claim depending on whether or not 'actual' is used by the inhabitants of each world to mean that world or whether there is or is not some metaphysically privileged world which alone is actual.) Then we can say that α is actually true iff $w_1 \in V_1(\alpha)$. But then we could equally define actual truth according as $1 \in V_2(\alpha)$. So if the criterion for semantical success is simply getting the right set of true sentences there seems nothing to choose between V_1 and V_2. But there is worse to come, in a way which was stressed in Putnam 1977. (And Putnam was referring to a lecture by Skolem in 1922 so the problem is a long-standing one.) Putnam makes use of a result from first-order predicate logic known as the Löwenheim–Skolem theorem. This says that any set of sentences of a first-order predicate language which can be simultaneously satisfied in any model (i.e. all made true together in an interpretation) can be simultaneously satisfied in an interpretation whose domain is no bigger than the class of natural numbers - even when some of these sentences in the intended interpretation say that the domain is larger than the class of natural numbers. It would not be profitable, especially for those unfamiliar with logic, to engage in a discussion of this result. Luckily it is not too difficult to shew how to have equivalent models, i.e. interpretations which make the same sentences true, which are not isomorphic.

Start once more with the 'intended' interpretation $\langle W_1, D_1, V_1 \rangle$, and form a new interpretation $\langle W_3, D_3, V_3 \rangle$ in the following way. The minimal change we can make is to give one of the members a shadow. Let a's shadow be referred to as $a^\star$. a's shadow can be anything we please, all that is required is that anything that a predicate of $\mathscr{L}$ says about a according to V_1, it also says about her shadow according to V_3. So

(1) $W_3 = W_1$ $\qquad\qquad$ $D_3 = \{a, a^\star, b\}$.

a's shadow does not have a name and the names of $\mathscr{L}$ all have the same values according to V_3 as according to V_1. Thus:

(2) $V_3(\textbf{\textit{Adriane}}) = a$
(3) $V_3(\textbf{\textit{Bruce}}) = b$

The predicates treat $a^\star$ just as if it were a herself. So

(4) $V_3(\textbf{\textit{runs}}) = \omega_1{}^+$

where $\omega_1{}^+$ is $\{\langle a, \{w_1\} \rangle, \langle a^\star, \{w_1\} \rangle, \langle b, \{w_2\} \rangle\}$

(5) $V_3(\textbf{\textit{see}}) = \omega_2{}^+$

where $\omega_2{}^+$ is

$\{\langle a,a,\emptyset \rangle, \langle a,a^\star,\emptyset \rangle, \langle a,\star,a,\emptyset \rangle, \langle a^\star,a^\star,\emptyset \rangle, \langle a,b,\{w_1\} \rangle, \langle a^\star,b,\{w_1\} \rangle, \langle b,a,\{w_2\} \rangle$,
$\langle b,a^\star,\{w_2\} \rangle, \langle b,b,\emptyset \rangle\}$

Examples (4) and (5) are each a bit of a mouthful but the idea is quite simple: where, and only where, you have a in ω_1 or in ω_2 you have in $\omega_1{}^+$ or $\omega_2{}^+$, $a^\star$ as well. The picture will make this clear.

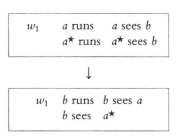

I hope I don't need to go through the proof that for any sentence α of $\mathscr{L}$,

(6) $V_1(\alpha) = V_3(\alpha)$

Since atomic sentences of $\mathscr{L}$ consist only of names and predicates, and since names have the same values in $\langle W_1, D_1, V_1 \rangle$ that they have in $\langle W_3, D_3, V_3 \rangle$ the atomic sentences all satisfy (6), and of course the sentential functors operate only on whole sentences and so preserve (6). The shadow example works in any categorial language provided that you re-interpret all the symbols so that where a symbol according to V_1 has a meaning which is a function which at some point involves a, V_3 will do the same thing for $a^\star$ as well, as we saw in the case of ω_1 and ω_1^+. The upshot of all this is that specifying which sentences are true is not sufficient to determine the intended interpretation of $\mathscr{L}$.

How can this problem be solved? It surely must be right that what makes a sentence be about running rather than numbers is a causal connection between language users and occasions of running. But how can we do this in a way which will lead to a possible-worlds semantics? The answer is surely to adopt a possible-worlds metaphysics, whereby language users are located in possible worlds and their properties and the relations they bear to one another will themselves be manufactured set-theoretically out of the very same set W of worlds, and D of individuals. In making this response I have been taking it that there is a truth of the matter about which interpretation is intended. Of course linguistic use is no doubt not sufficient to pick out just one interpretation. Most words have vague boundaries especially in application to remote and unlikely situations, so it is an idealization to suggest that we can get just one interpretation. Nevertheless the individuals, worlds and so on are intended to represent what is out there. This makes $\langle W_1, D_1, V_1 \rangle$ right as against $\langle W_2, D_2, V_2 \rangle$ for all that they are isomorphic.

There is another way of looking at interpretations, a way that is suggested in Kaplan 1978. Kaplan speaks of interpretations as models and one feature he takes seriously is that the intrinsic nature of the elements of a model is irrelevant to their semantical use. Thus, says Kaplan (1978 p. 97), an entity which is a unicorn in a model may in reality be Professor Hintikka. Applied to $\langle W_1, D_1, V_1 \rangle$ and $\langle W_2, D_2, V_2 \rangle$ this means that instead of saying that a *is* Adriane and b is Bruce we say that in $\langle W_1, D_1, V_1 \rangle$ a *represents* Adriane and b *represents* Bruce, while in $\langle W_2, D_2, V_2 \rangle$ 3 represents Adriane and 4 represents Bruce. If we look at things in this way then indeed it doesn't matter whether we use $\langle W_1,D_1,V_1 \rangle$ or $\langle W_2,D_2,V_2 \rangle$. The task of semantics proper would then be restricted to explaining those properties of linguistic expressions which depend only on the structure of an interpretation. i.e., properties such that a certain sentence is true in every world (where the 'worlds' of $\langle W,D,V \rangle$ are just the members of W, whatever they are) or that a sentence α entails a sentence β in the sense that $V(\alpha) \subseteq V(\beta)$, and so on. These facts are preserved by isomorphic interpretations, and indeed by some interpretations which are not isomorphic.

The problem with this way of looking at interpretations is that it emerges that semantics is not doing what we thought it was. For the whole point of interpreting $\mathscr{L}$ by such things as assigning Adriane to **Adriane** is to shew how language connects up with the world. But if $a \in$ D, which we had previously supposed *was* Adriane, now only represents her then the semantic relation is still unexplained. For the question is what it is to represent Adriane. This seems to me similar to, if not the same as, the problem which exercises chapter 3 of Lewis 1986a. Lewis is concerned to defend his brand of modal realism against those who make worlds out of other things. While much of what he says is concerned with the ontological status of these 'ersatz' entities, some at least of his arguments are addressed to those who claim that these entities aren't worlds, they just represent worlds. The argument against such claims is that we now have to know what representing is. I agree with this part of Lewis's attack on ersatzism, but it will need to be defended against what Putnam says in Putnam 1977. (Putnam is actually concerned with the problem of how non-isomorphic interpretations can verify just the same sentences. He seems to think that the isomorphism problem is trivial, though a remark about cats and dogs at the very end of the paper suggests that even isomorphic interpretations might raise the same problem.) If we think about $\langle W_1,D_1,V_1 \rangle$ and $\langle W_2,D_2,V_2 \rangle$ we can make Putnam's point in the following way:

In order to tell you about the difference between $\langle W_1,D_1,V_1 \rangle$ and $\langle W_2,D_2,V_2 \rangle$ I must use a metalanguage. In that metalanguage I use symbols like 'a' or '3'. But the very same argument that was used against the distinction between $\langle W_1,D_1,V_1 \rangle$ and $\langle W_2,D_2,V_2 \rangle$ can be used to shew that our metalanguage cannot distinguish between a and 3. Putnam is concerned to use this argument against causal solutions to the isomorphism problem. A causal solution to the problem of $\langle W_1,D_1,V_1 \rangle$ and $\langle W_2,D_2,V_2 \rangle$ is one which says that $\langle W_1,D_1,V_1 \rangle$ is right and

$\langle W_2, D_2, V_2 \rangle$ wrong because there are appropriate causal links between speakers' utterances of sentences involving **Adriane, Bruce, runs** and **sees** and the entities a, b, ω_1 and ω_2, which do not hold between these utterances and 3, 4, $\omega_1^\star$ and $\omega_2^\star$. But, Putnam would say, any interpretation for a metalanguage which describes the links between speakers and a, b, ω_1 and ω_2 can be replaced by an equivalent interpretation in which the statement that these links hold now says that they hold between 3, 4, $\omega_1^\star$ and $\omega_2^\star$.

What can we say about this? A realist like Lewis will simply say that speakers and their properties and relations, including relations to the words they speak, are simply *there* as part of reality. We may need a metalanguage to *say* that they are there, but whether or not we say so they just *do* stand in appropriate causal relations to a, b, ω_1 and ω_2 that they do not stand in to 3, 4, $\omega_1^\star$ and $\omega_2^\star$. (For Lewis's views on Putnam see Lewis 1984.) Such a view is also, I *think*, held in chapter 5 of Montague 1974, and I have some sympathy with it. Putnam thinks differently. Putnam thinks that it is a mistake to suppose that models are 'lost noumenal waifs looking for someone to name them'; rather 'they are constructions within our theory itself, and they have names from birth'. But even if we accept this, it does not really change the semantic problem. We invoke Quine's (1969) doctrine of ontological relativity. Suppose that some way or other we have an interpretation for our metalanguage in which there are people and they stand in certain relations and have certain properties. The fact that there could be *other* isomorphic interpretations is now irrelevant. They have dropped out of the picture. The isomorphism problem is this: according to the intended interpretation to our metalanguage there are people in various possible worlds using the language $\mathcal{L}$. Assume that u is one of these worlds. Within the interpretation to the metalanguage we may speak of interpretations to $\mathcal{L}$. Assume that $\langle W_1, D_1, V_1 \rangle$ and $\langle W_2, D_2, V_2 \rangle$ are isomorphic. Then, if all we require is that the set of sentences of $\mathcal{L}$ which are true in the 'world' of $\langle W_1, D_1, V_1 \rangle$ or $\langle W_2, D_2, V_2 \rangle$ which is designated as the actual world correspond to the sentences of $\mathcal{L}$ which are true in u as used by speakers of $\mathcal{L}$ in u, then $\langle W_1, D_1, V_1 \rangle$ and $\langle W_2, D_2, V_2 \rangle$ cannot be distinguished. Now this problem *can* be solved by a causal theory. For the distinction between $\langle W_1, D_1, V_1 \rangle$ and $\langle W_2, D_2, V_2 \rangle$ is now being made *within* a particular interpretation to the metalanguage, and within that interpretation there will be appropriate causal relations which hold between the speakers of $\mathcal{L}$ in u and $\langle W_1, D_1, V_1 \rangle$ which do not hold between those speakers and $\langle W_2, D_2, V_2 \rangle$. For instance, even ignoring V_1 and V_2, if $\langle W_1, D_1, V_1 \rangle$ is the right interpretation then W_1 ought to contain the very same worlds as are in the background metalinguistic model, and D_1 ought to contain the very same individuals. So, whether or not we are realists the isomorphism problem for semantics can be solved using a causal theory of meaning.

The isomorphism problem, as I understand it, is that a purely model-theoretic approach to semantics will not by itself give you an account of what constitutes the correct structure, even relative to a particular account (in a possible-worlds structure) of the behaviour of language users. This is not of course a *criticism* of model-theoretic semantics since the latter does not pretend to solve this problem. Still it can hardly be a brute fact that one model is right and another wrong. I hope it is almost a truism that *in some sense* the correct semantic structure is determined by a pattern of causal interaction between the utterance of sentences and facts in the world. What is less of a truism is any particular account of just what this interaction is. For instance, the truism does *not* claim that the meaning of a particular utterance is determined by the causal relations entered into by the utterance. For it may be that what a particular utterance means is determined by the causal properties of other utterances of it and other sentences. Thus, the truism is compatible with a holistic view of meaning, and claims merely that whether or not a particular $\langle W, D, V \rangle$ is the correct one can depend on the totality of causal interactions within the speech community.

In moving from $\langle W_1, D_1, V_1 \rangle$ to $\langle W_2, D_2, V_2 \rangle$ the set of worlds W_2 was changed even though isomorphism was preserved. For that reason the values of sentences of $\mathscr{L}$, although corresponding, cannot be exactly the same. We can get an intermediate case by having an interpretation $\langle W_4, D_4, V_4 \rangle$ in which $W_4 = W_1$, $D_4 = D_2$, and V_4 is defined so that

$$V_4(\textbf{\textit{Adriane}}) = 3$$
$$V_4(\textbf{\textit{Bruce}}) = 4$$
$$V_4(\textbf{\textit{runs}}) = \omega_1'$$
$$V_4(\textbf{\textit{sees}}) = \omega_2'$$

where

$$\omega_1' = \{\langle 3, \{w_1\}\rangle, \langle 4, \{w_2\}\rangle, \langle 4, 3, \{w_2\}\rangle, \langle 4, 4, \emptyset\rangle\}$$

If we think of this pictorially we may suppose that in w_1 there are 3 French hens while in w_2 there are 4. Suppose that in w_1 3 arrows miss 4 targets while in w_2 4 arrows miss 3 targets. Then if

$\Omega_1'(n)$ means 'n is the number of French hens'

and

$\Omega_2'(n,m)$ means 'n arrows missed m targets'

we have the following picture

$$\boxed{\quad 1 \quad \Omega_1'(3) \quad \Omega_2'(3,4) \quad}$$

$$\downarrow$$

$$\boxed{\quad 2 \quad \Omega_1'(4) \quad \Omega_2'(4,3) \quad}$$

What this means is that for any sentence α of $\mathscr{L}$ we have

$V_1(\alpha) = V_4(\alpha)$

In particular such sentences as

(7) **Adriane runs**

or

(8) **Bruce sees Adriane**

will come out as being true in exactly the same worlds even though in $\langle W_2, D_1, V_1 \rangle$ they report facts about Adriane and Bruce, while in $\langle W_4, D_4, V_4 \rangle$ they report facts about numbers. This version of the isomorphism problem is important because it shews that any causal account of what it is for the expressions of a language of a population to mean what they do cannot rest content on connecting up utterances with the truth conditions of whole sentences, for they can come to have those very same truth conditions in many different ways.

If we are to put language users into the worlds it will not come amiss to be more specific about our metaphysics. The metaphysics I favour can be approached initially by looking at some options presented in Kaplan 1975. Kaplan lists four metaphysical positions depending on (a) whether one is a possibilist or an actualist and (b) whether one is a haecceitist or an anti-haecceitist. I shall explore, with a view to endorsing, the possibilist haecceitist option. I will not actually argue for the position although I hope to clear away a number of misconceptions which might stand in the way of accepting it. Kaplan cites Richard Montague as holding this view, and a reading of chapter 5 of Montague 1974 inclines me to think that he is correct in so doing. My own work over the years has adopted Montague's framework, but without explicitly considering it in relation to other ways of construing the metaphysics of possible worlds. This has mostly not mattered and I am inclined to think that the views are all intertranslatable, so that even now I am not really bothered about which of Kaplan's positions one should adopt. So it's perhaps best to think of what I am going to do as shewing that the Montague option isn't so silly as has sometimes been thought. I say this because it does seem that relatively few authors have explicitly adopted it, and it, rather curiously, seems a forgotten option in explicit metaphysical discussion, even though it is probably the most common framework assumed by practitioners of analyses using possible worlds in the formal semantics of natural language.

In order to keep the discussion specific I shall set out a particular view of the kind Kaplan might have in mind. Whether it really is what he had in mind, and whether this or that philosopher holds it will be of less importance. For that reason I shall not actually use the names 'possibilism' or 'haecceitism' for the view I am about to describe but, since its most essential feature is that it refuses to make it a metaphysical question whether the very same individual can appear in more than one world, I shall call it *transmundism*. A transmundist metaphysical theory may be specified as follows. First of all there is the class W of *possible worlds*. As I intend to use the term, transmundism *per se* is neutral on the question of what precisely a possible world is. This is one of the reasons why the word 'possibilism' may be inappropriate. Michael Loux (1979, p. 60) cites a view I once put forward, as an example of non-modal actualism, on the grounds that its possible worlds were made up out of space–time points. That view would certainly count as a transmundist view as I intend to use the term. So of course would a view which says that possible worlds are real things on their own account, and not to be made up from things in this world.

The second feature of transmundism is that it assumes a class or domain D of 'things'. I wanted to say 'individuals' but that might be understood too restrictively. D can be anything we want to talk about. Transmundism as such has nothing to say about what can be in D. It is even allowed, and by some required, that $W \subseteq D$. I once suggested that ordinary concrete individuals are functions from worlds to sets of space–time points, each such set being the 'manifestation' of that individual in that world. Such an account is permitted, though not required, by transmundism. I shall assume that all the entities needed in a semantics based on a transmundist framework are to be constructed set-theoretically out of W and D. This is partly for convenience and definiteness, since there are alternatives to set-theory whose use would make little difference to the philosophical points I wish to make. But it is not entirely so. For instance a metaphysics taking as basic and unanalysed the notion of a property or relation, and using this notion in analysing subject–predicate sentences, might well not be a transmundist theory. Transmundism, as I shall construe it, is neutral on the question of whether complex set-theoretical entities are in D or not. The metaphysics of Cresswell 1973 puts them into D. The price of doing this is that you cannot make use of functions whose domain is the whole of D since if the axiom of foundation is assumed a function in D whose domain was D would have to have itself as one of its arguments.

One of the crucial features of transmundism has already crept in, almost by accident, and that is that nothing at all has been said about whether the members of D are understood to be only actual individuals or to allow merely possible individuals. In so far as the distinction is appropriate the choice of a single domain means that D must include possible as well as actual individuals, but one of the points I am going to go on to make is that the distinction is not one which should be drawn at the ontological level. This may seem paradoxical in that if the distinction between an individual which is actual and one which is merely possible is not an ontological one it is surely hard to say what is. Nevertheless it will, I hope, emerge that, paradoxical or not, that is what transmundism claims.

Things have properties and stand in relation to one another. Transmundism analyses these set-theoretically. One may either speak of a relation as a many-place property, or one may speak of a property as a one-place relation. Either way an n-place property (or relation) can be analysed as an n-place function from members of D to subsets of W. If you call a subset of W a proposition then an n-place property takes n individuals (in some particular order) into a proposition. If we denote such a property by ω then for $a_1,...,a_n \in D$, $a_1,...,a_n$ have the property ω in world w if $w \in \omega(a_1,...,a_n)$. Equivalently an n-place property could be a function which associates with each $w \in W$ a set of n-tuples from D. That set is often called the extension of ω in w and is the things that have the property, in relation to one another, in world w. I said equivalently, but that is not quite correct, for if we allow partial functions the former way will permit a property to be undefined for certain individuals, but if it is defined it will hold or not hold determinately in each world. The latter way will permit a property to be undefined at a certain world, but if it is defined at that world, it will be determinate for every n-tuple from D whether or not that n-tuple is in the extension of the property at that world. The former way seems closer to natural language, but the two are equivalent where defined, and it is certainly convenient to use the word 'extension' for the things which satisfy the property in a given world. The word 'extension' contrasts with 'intension', which refers to the property itself.

I began by suggesting that the metaphysical framework that I was going to present was a version of possibilism and haecceitism. I have adopted the name transmundism because as far as I am aware it is not a name already in use, and the fact is that its key feature is not so much to take sides on questions like possibilism versus actualism as to maintain that in transmundism many questions which are often thought to be metaphysical turn out not to be. Indeed some may feel that transmundism is not a metaphysical doctrine at all, but is rather a framework within which metaphysical positions can be stated. Perhaps anyone who uses possible worlds is a transmundist. But if all possible-worlds theorists are transmundists then some transmundists make more restrictive assumptions than others, and would, I suspect, rule out as impossible options which transmundism as such regards as equally metaphysically viable. More of this in chapter 5.

Typically, after setting up a domain W of possible worlds, and a domain D of things, D is divided into a system of subsets by a function which associates with each w some $D_w \subseteq D$. $\cup\{D_w : w \in W\} = D$, and D_w is considered as the things which 'exist' or are 'actual' in w. Often indeed the D_w's are introduced first and D is simply *defined* as $\cup\{D_w : w \in W\}$. In a transmundist structure this division is not initially given, and there are as many ways of dividing up D as there are functions from W to $\mathscr{P}D$. If we do choose to single out one of these functions there are various options in what we may require it to satisfy. One might require, as David Lewis at least would for 'ordinary' individuals, that if $w \neq w'$ then $D_w \cap D_{w'} = \emptyset$. Or one might require that $D_w = D_{w'}$ for all $w, w' \in D$, if you think that there cannot be worlds containing different individuals from this one. Given a collection of D_w's there will be a one-place property ω_{actual} such that for any $a \in D$ and for any $w \in W$, $w \in \omega_{actual}(a)$ iff $a \in D_w{}'$. ω_{actual} is the property of actually existing. I hope that the sense in which the ontological significance of actual existence is not important might already be emerging. For given *any* one-place predicate ω, we may form a system of domains based on ω in which $D(\omega)_w$ is just the set of things which satisfy ω in w. That is, $D(\omega)_w = \{a{:}w \in \omega(a)\}$.

What then is the property of existing, and how does it enter into the semantics of natural language? If we consider what kind of things might be said to exist in one world but not in another, we find I believe that they are all things which have spatio-temporal location. I possess a copy of *Counterfactuals*. It is currently (2 March 1990) in my room in Hughes House. That is its location. At every moment during the last sixteen or so years it has had a spatial location and I trust it will continue to have one for many more years. But there was a time when it had no spatial location, and there will presumably be a time at which it will again have no spatial location. I have no account to offer of what it is for something to have a certain spatial location at a certain time, but it is clear to me that many things do, and equally clear to me that we say that those things exist at those times and in those places.

It is often thought that there is an important metaphysical distinction between abstract and concrete entities, and that this difference is manifested in the fact that while abstract entities have necessary existence concrete entities typically do not. I shall shew that in a transmundist framework this distinction turns out not to be a metaphysical one. In Cresswell 1973 I suggested that ordinary individuals, like my copy of *Counterfactuals*, might be thought of as functions from possible worlds to their 'manifestations', where these are the sets of spatio-temporal locations they occupy in the world in question. This notion of individual is no doubt too simple-minded for plausibility, but it will do to shew how transmundism eliminates the metaphysical significance of the abstract/concrete distinction. It has seemed an important question to some whether worlds themselves are abstract or concrete. In the model I am alluding to worlds were taken as sets of space–time points. So ordinary individuals are functions from sets of space–time points to sets of space–time points. Such functions look like abstract things; but now suppose that ω_{actual} is a function whose domain consists entirely of functions f such that f is a function from worlds to sets of space–time points. And suppose that $w \in \omega_{actual}(f)$ iff $f(w) \neq \emptyset$. In other words existence is taken to be having a non-empty spatio-temporal location just as I suggested. Then these functions, whether abstract or concrete, will exist in some worlds but not in others.

So the position we have reached is this. Among the properties admitted by a transmundist structure $\langle W,D \rangle$ there is one that we might call ω_{actual}, whose domain is the class of all things whose existence may be said to be contingent. These are things that occupy spatio-temporal locations in various worlds (whether or not they are analysed as functions from worlds to manifestations). For such an $a \in D$, and $w \in W$, $w \in \omega_{actual}(a)$ iff a's spatio-temporal location in w is non-empty. Relative to such an ω_{actual} any n-place property ω may be said to be *existence-entailing* in its k'th place iff, for $a_1,...,a_n \in D$, and $1 \leqslant k \leqslant n$, and $w \in W$, if

$$w \in \omega(a_1,...,a_n) \text{ then } w \in \omega_{actual}(a_k)$$

Whether or not a property is existence-entailing is relative to some particular ω_{actual} and the ontological status of ω as a construct in $\langle W,D \rangle$ is unaffected. This is what I mean by saying that in an important sense transmundism does not treat existence as a metaphysical phenomenon.

An important feature of transmundism is that it does not require that all properties be existence-entailing. Indeed how could it since in a transmundist structure existence emerges as just one property among others? Nevertheless, it could well turn out that most of the properties that we ordinarily attribute to things are existence-entailing. If I say that my copy of *Counterfactuals* has a blue dust jacket, I attribute to it something which, if true, is true just at those times at which the book has a spatial location. Not though just at these places. If I say that *Counterfactuals* is in the furthest bookshelf, that must be true at time t and place p iff *Counterfactuals* at t is in the furthest bookshelf from p, and in that case p will *not* be the spatial location of *Counterfactuals*. In certain cases the same can occur with time. The time at which a sunspot is visible on earth will be later than the time at which whatever it is in the sun which causes the sunspot occurs. Predicates which are existence-entailing in this sense are also existence-entailing modally. If my copy of *Counterfactuals* has a blue cover in world w then it has a spatial location in w.

The account of existence that I am offering makes reference to time and space. They are however treated differently, and I suspect that, whatever physics may tell us, natural language does treat them differently. In particular, even if most of the properties expressed by phrases of natural language are existence-entailing in the temporal and the modal sense, in

that a thing which has a property in a world at a time is located
somewhere in that world at that time, yet it is not as a rule located where
it has the property. So times ought to enter into the discussions of
properties in a way similar to worlds. One way in which this can be done
in a transmundist framework is to make W the set of all world–time pairs.
That I believe is the best approach in natural-language semantics. Where
the temporal argument plays no role I shall usually pretend it doesn't
exist. As far as transmundism goes any function from things to sets of
worlds is a property, and on that view there are just as many which are
not existence-entailing as are existence-entailing. But this metaphysical
fact does not prevent from being existence-entailing most of those
properties which we find sufficiently useful to refer to by expressions of
natural language. This is not surprising or mysterious. We ourselves are
beings having to live in a spatio-temporal world. What wonder that a
thing's spatio-temporal location is of the highest importance to us?

Given such a metaphysics based on W and D, among the members of
D are the users of a language $\mathscr{L}$. The intended interpretation of $\mathscr{L}$ will
presumably use the same W and D on which the metaphysics is based.
This would immediately rule out $\langle W_2, D_2, V_2 \rangle$ but it would not rule out
$\langle W_4, D_4, V_4 \rangle$. In later chapters I shall consider various strategies for
determining which interpretation is the correct one.

4

Quantification

The purpose of this chapter is twofold. First I shall shew how to extend $\mathcal{L}$ to include quantification and variable-binding, and then I shall look at the question of whether the quantifiers should be interpreted possibilistically or actualistically. A language like $\mathcal{L}$ is usually extended by symbols which mean 'every' and 'some'. These are called *quantifiers* and are customarily represented by $\forall$ and $\exists$. We also extend the category of *names* to include *individual variables* usually written as x, y, z,...,etc. As far as formation rules go individual variables are treated exactly as **Adriane**, **Bruce**, etc. The new formation rule is

> FR6   If α is a sentence and x is an individual variable then $\forall x\alpha$ is a sentence.

(The terminology of FR6 differs slightly from standard usage in that the word 'sentence' in quantificational logic is sometimes used a little more restrictively.)

An example of a sentence requiring FR6 is

(1) $\forall x$ *x* **whistles**

Example (1) is interpreted as meaning 'everyone whistles'. More literally (1) can be read as: for every value of x

(2)   *x* **whistles**

is true.

Calling x a variable means that its value is not fixed once and for all, even in a given interpretation $\langle W, D, V \rangle$. Rather, we add to an interpretation a value-assignment to all the individual variables. If v is such an assignment then for any variable x, v assigns to x a member of D; i.e. $v(x) \in D$. The interpretation now gives values to all expressions with respect to some v. We write $V_v(\alpha)$ to denote the value that V gives to α

when its variables have been given their values by v. We make this precise as follows:

(3)   If α is any symbol except a variable then $V_v(\alpha) = V(\alpha)$.
(4)   If x is a variable then $V_v(x) = v(x)$.
(5)   If δ is in category $(\sigma/\tau_1...\tau_n)$ and $\alpha_1,..., \alpha_n$ are, respectively, in categories $\tau_1,...,\tau_n$, then

$$V_v(\delta\alpha_1...\alpha_n) = V_v(\delta)(V_v(\alpha_1),...,V_v(\alpha_n))$$

These rules are no more than the ones in the last chapter, but with the values for variables coming from v, and V_v representing values depending on both V and v. FR6 requires something different. The idea is that $V_v(\forall x\alpha)$ will be true in a world w provided α itself is true whatever x is assigned. But look at a sentence like

(6) $\forall x$ x *sees* y.

In order to decide whether $w \in V_v(6)$ we have to know whether

(7) x *sees* y

is true for every value of x. But what about y? v will give y a value, and we don't want *that* to change when we look at other values for x. So we are not interested in *all* possible assignments, only those which are just like v for all variables besides x, though they may give any value they please to x. So call an assignment μ an *x-alternative* of v iff, for every variable y, except, possibly, x, $\mu(y) = v(y)$. Then

(8) $w \in V_v(\forall x\alpha)$ iff, for every x-alternative μ of v, $w \in V_\mu(\alpha)$.

It is convenient at this point to introduce standard logical symbols for *not*, *if* and *and*. I shall use $\sim$, $\supset$ and &. For *or* I shall use V. (This is the *inclusive or*. α V β is true provided at least one of α and β is true.) We may define $\exists x$ as $\sim\forall x\sim$. Whether we do that or not the meaning of $\exists$ is expressed by

(9) $w \in V_v(\exists x\alpha)$ iff there is an x-alternative μ of v such that $w \in V_\mu(\alpha)$.

Both (8) and (9) are stated without reference to any 'existence property' of the kind discussed on page 45, so it is clear that $\forall$ and $\exists$ are interpreted possibilistically in the sense that $V_v(\forall x\alpha)$ would be false at w if $w \notin V_\mu(\alpha)$ even if $w \notin \omega_{actual}(\mu(x))$, i.e. for $\forall x\alpha$ to be true in a world α must be true for all x's, including those which do not exist in w. Analogously $\exists x\alpha$ will be true in w if there is at least one x which satisfies α, even one which does not exist in w. An actualist quantifier would be interpreted by saying that

$w \in V_\nu(\forall x\alpha)$ iff $w \in V_\mu(\alpha)$ for every μ which is just like ν except possibly in assignment to $\mu(x)$, provided $w \in \omega_{actual}(\mu(x))$, and $w \in V_\nu(\exists x\alpha)$ iff $w \in V_\mu(\alpha)$ for some μ exactly like ν except possibly in assignment to x provided $w \in \omega_{actual}(\mu(x))$.

The first comment I wish to make is that in the framework I called *transmundism* on page 43 it cannot be a *metaphysical* issue whether or not the quantifiers are interpreted possibilistically or actualistically. This seems to me important since the question of whether we quantify over possibilia often *is* presented as a metaphysical matter. Given that it is a semantical matter then the only substantive question will be whether quantification in natural language is to be interpreted possibilistically or actualistically. My aim will be to shew that *if it matters* then the quantifiers have to be interpreted possibilistically.

The logician's quantifiers are not the quantifiers of ordinary language. In ordinary language we say things like 'every chair is taken', or 'there is a seat by the window'. Even when we try to express $\forall x$ or $\exists x$ in natural language we say things like 'everything is F' or 'something is F', and while 'everything' and 'something' are both single words it is clear that the word 'thing' has a role to play. (Notice the difference between 'everything' and 'everyone'.)

Natural-language quantifiers are in fact two-place operators (see e.g. Cresswell 1973, pp. 135f., or Barwise and Cooper 1981), where the first place is filled by a simple or complex common-noun expression, and the second place by a verb phrase. (This is not strictly grammatically correct; what happens is that a determiner turns a common-noun expression into a noun phrase, which combines with a verb phrase to form a sentence.) We may think of sentences of the form

$\forall x(\alpha,\beta)$ and $\exists x(\alpha,\beta)$

which mean, respectively, every α satisfies β and some α satisfies β. From the point of view of logic no harm is done by expressing these in the usual way as $\forall x(\alpha \supset \beta)$ and $\exists x(\alpha \mathbin{\&} \beta)$ though it must be remembered that there are non-standard quantifiers like **most** which do not yield to this treatment. If $\forall$ and $\exists$ are interpreted possibilistically then it is not at all difficult to see that actualist quantifiers can be defined, simply by restricting the possibilist quantifiers by a predicate, say A, such that $V(A) = \omega_{actual}$. Every actual α satisfies β becomes

(10) $\forall x((Ax \mathbin{\&} \alpha) \supset \beta)$

and 'some actual α satisfies β' becomes

(11) $\exists x((Ax \ \& \ \alpha) \ \& \ \beta)$

Now suppose that α is a predicate which expresses, with respect to a variable x, an existence-entailing property in the sense that, where ω is the function such that for μ like ν except that $\mu(x) = a$, $w \in \omega(a)$ iff $w \in V_\mu(\alpha)$ then ω is existence-entailing. For short, call such predicates existence-entailing predicates. Suppose that α in (10) and (11) is one. That is, suppose that where ν is any assignment to the variables of $\mathscr{L}$ then where μ is just like ν except possibly at x, $V_\mu(\alpha) \subseteq \omega_{actual}(\mu(x))$.

If α has this property, then given that $V(A) = \omega_{actual}$ it is immediate that

(12) $V_\mu(Ax \ \& \ \alpha) = V_\mu(\alpha)$

Since this is true for any value μ may give to x then we have that (10) and (11) are respectively true in precisely the same worlds as (13) and (14):

(13) $\forall x(\alpha \supset \beta)$
(14) $\exists x(\alpha \ \& \ \beta)$

Now in natural language (at least in English) α will be represented by a noun phrase, and this means that there are certain restrictions on what α can be. Suppose it seemed plausible that such an α was always existence-entailing. One reason that might stop this is negation. For suppose that for every $a \in D$, $\omega(a) \subseteq \omega_{actual}(a)$, and suppose there is some $b \in D$ and some $w \in W$ such that $w \notin \omega_{actual}(b)$. Then $w \notin \omega(b)$ and so $w \in \omega_{not}(b)$ and so ω_{not} is not existence-entailing. If we assume that *not* behaves classically then if a predicate is existence-entailing its negation is not. (See Salmon 1987.) But a noun phrase cannot be negated, at least not by the word *not* (except in a relative clause, which restricts a previously given unnegated common-noun expression). Common nouns can be negated by the prefix 'non' but it is much less certain that 'non' behaves as classical negation. A candle which has completely burnt away may be said to be no longer a candle, but to call it a non-candle seems to suggest that it still exists somewhere though not as a candle. I am not absolutely sure that this is so but if it is the case that simple or complex noun phrases are always existence-entailing in natural language then there is no difference between (10) and (13) or between (11) and (14), and so no linguistic fact which could tell us whether the quantifiers are interpreted possibilistically or actualistically.

Traditional wisdom in recent philosophy tells us that existence is expressed by the existential quantifier. Why else is it so called? Terminology doesn't worry me. Like Quine I am happy to give the word 'exists' to whoever wants it. The crucial feature of transmundism is that, in addition to the quantifiers which range over the whole of D, there are predicates which for a certain subclass of D mark off a property which might be called existence. At this point it might be worth calling the temporal parallel to mind, since what is frequently held to be absurd in the modal case is mostly happily accepted in the temporal case. In ordinary discourse I believe we are quite happy to say that Socrates no longer exists. A very few philosophers – Arthur Prior is perhaps the most prominent example (see Prior and Fine 1977) – have been prepared to say that from the current non-existence of Socrates we cannot infer that there is something which no longer exists. That is because he took seriously the present tense of *is* in 'there is'. So for Prior

(15) $\exists x \; x$ does not now exist

is always false. As I said, most philosophers are happy to accept (15) on the ground that $\exists$ is interpreted tenselessly to range over things from all times. The reason for this I believe is that if your semantics has a domain of entities of a certain kind then your language ought to have a quantifier which ranges over them all. In fact if you turn this principle on its head you get Quine's criterion of ontological commitment. Your domain of entities is precisely what you quantify over. Quine of course rejects quantification over possibilia, but that is because he rejects possible worlds in the first place. Indeed I suspect Quine's objection to transmundism would be that if you have a domain of possibilia then you will have to quantify over them, and that is what is objectionable. I am not concerned to defend transmundism against those who reject possible worlds in any form, particularly those who reject the whole idea of logical modality. I am trying to shew that if you accept transmundism in the first place, then there is nothing to stop you interpreting the quantifiers possibilistically.

Suppose that α is an existence-entailing predicate. Then it is clear that 'there are α's' or even 'α's exist' can be equally formalized as $\exists x(Ax \; \& \; \alpha)$ or as $\exists x\alpha$. Further 'all α's exist' will be translated as $\forall x(\alpha \supset Ax)$, but since α is existence-entailing, this will be a necessary truth, and similarly 'some α's don't exist', $\exists x(\alpha \; \& \sim Ax)$, will come out as logically impossible.

When I began work on this topic it seemed to me obvious that almost every common noun of natural language is existence-entailing. And if, as

I suggested above, where α is a noun non-α is a noun which is also existence-entailing, then almost every noun phrase will be existence-entailing, and so almost every natural-language quantifier will be restricted by an existence-entailing predicate. And I have just shewn that for such predicates you get the same truth conditions whether the quantifiers are interpreted possibilistically or actualistically. That is one reason why the existential quantifier has been thought to be all you need to express actual existence. However what it really means is that there can be no *direct* arguments from natural language in favour of actualist quantifiers. The reason is this. If all noun phrases are existence-entailing then (10) and (11) will be equivalent, respectively, to (13) and (14). So to shew that quantifiers have to be interpreted actualistically we must produce a noun phrase α which is not existence-entailing. But what would it take to do *this*? We would need to shew that it is possible for something to be α without existing. That is, we would need to shew the truth of

$$M \exists x(\alpha \;\&\; \sim Ax)$$

But the defender of actualism is committed to the view that

$$\exists x(\alpha \;\&\; \sim Ax)$$

is a logical falsehood. So the defender of actualism can produce no evidence that quantifiers must be interpreted actualistically.

The actualist must resort at this point to an indirect argument. The indirect argument is that the onus of proof is on the defender of possibilism. If a possibilist and an actualist interpretation of the quantifiers always result in the same truth conditions for natural-language quantification sentences then actualism is to be preferred as having a weaker commitment. In fact I think this is a good reply, and I agree that the possibilist is under an obligation to shew that there are things we need to say that can only be said using possibilist quantifiers. I and others have tried to do this elsewhere and I shall not do it here because my purpose is not to argue *for* transmundism except in the sense of trying to address arguments against it.

I said a while back that I used to think that most nouns were existence-entailing. I am less sure than I used to be about whether this is true for natural-kind terms, and so my approach will be to shew that possibilist quantification poses no threat whether or not they are. The best way to approach this is via a discussion of mythical entities. We all know that there are no fairies, centaurs, unicorns or flying horses. It might initially seem that that shews that these predicates are not existence-entailing. But actually it shews, at least *prima facie*, the opposite. For it is only if these predicates *are* existence-entailing that we can symbolize the statements of non-existence by formulae like

$\sim\exists x(x$ is a fairy$)$

and the like. For if 'fairy' is not existence-entailing and $\exists$ is a possibilist quantifier then $\exists x(x$ is a fairy$)$ could be true because there is a non-existent fairy.

Although there are no flying horses there are certainly horses but if **horse** is an existence-entailing predicate then so is ***flying horse***. The argument that **horse** is not existence-entailing is simple. If it *is* existence-entailing then

(16) Pegasus is a flying horse

will be false. But surely it is true. This objection is not decisive, since I will shew presently how to accommodate the fact that (16) is literally false. A stronger argument might be this. Suppose that horses are an endangered species, and to protect them we have gathered them together. We wonder whether they are all here and someone says:

(17) At least one horse isn't here.

Could this be held to be true on the ground that Pegasus isn't here? If it could then **horse** is not existence-entailing. (The verb phrase in (17) is negated because 'is here' must be taken to be an existence-entailing predicate and if we take negation classically in a transmundist model we have that 'isn't here' is therefore not existence-entailing.) Natural-kind terms like **horse** have sometimes been held to denote essential properties. An essential property has usually been held to be a property which a thing has, if it has it at all, in every world in which it exists. This is on the ground that if you define an essential property to be one which a thing has, if it has it at all, necessarily, then only necessary existents will have essential properties. But if the property in question is not existence-entailing this does not follow. Suppose that **horse** is an essential predicate but is not existence-entailing. Then Pegasus will be a horse in every world, even though he doesn't exist in every world.

Although I am less sure than I once was that words like **horse** *are* existence-entailing and although I find some compulsion in arguments based on (16) and (17), I do not think they are completely watertight. For suppose *horse* is existence-entailing. Then (16) is false. But so what? A person uttering (16) is engaged in telling a story from Greek mythology; perhaps such a person is not pretending that (16) is true. What you are being asked to do is to listen to (16) in order to explore imaginatively, and enjoy thinking about, a world in which it *is* true. And in that world Pegasus *does* exist.

To the fountain of Pirene, therefore, people's great grandfathers had been in the habit of going (as long as they were youthful, and retained their faith in winged horses), in hopes of getting a glimpse of the beautiful Pegasus. But of late years he had been very seldom seen. Indeed, there were many of the country folks, dwelling within an hour's walk of the fountain, who had never beheld Pegasus, and did not believe that there was any such creature in existence.

Well, these disbelievers in Pegasus, were they right or were they wrong? If some philosophers had their way the disbelievers would be right, for, as we know, there are no winged horses, and Pegasus didn't exist. But of course the solution is very simple. For Pegasus does exist in the possible world of that piece of mythology, and so the disbelievers are wrong. The world in which they do their disbelieving is a world in which Pegasus *does* exist. Of course they have their own belief worlds. For the world as they conceive it to be does not contain Pegasus.

Alternatively you may say that when we call (16) true we mean to claim that it is true in Greek mythology rather than true in the actual world, and 'it is true in Greek mythology that' acts as an intensional operator. This becomes especially plausible when a mythical character has a factual origin. Thus one might say that in legend Robin Hood robbed the rich to help the poor but that in actual fact he was nothing but a bandit. Also there might be different stories. I once read a detective story which suggested that Dr Jekyll and Mr Hyde really were two people. So the sentence

(18) Dr Jekyll is Mr Hyde

would have different truth value according to different stories.

One way in which nouns can be modified is by adding the word *possible*. Quine's famous passage ridiculing possibilist quantification makes great play with this word. But in fact, if we bear in mind the lessons learnt so far it should not prove too troublesome. In 1987 I was approached by the then Dean of Arts in Wellington with a view to becoming his successor. Luckily I could plead that I was negotiating with the University of Massachusetts with a view to spending several months of each year in Amherst, which would make it difficult to undertake the duties of Dean. I suppose therefore that there is a sense in which I am a possible Dean. So if I ask

(19) How many possible Deans are present?

the answer is that there is at least one and most likely several. No doubt it is a vague matter just who counts as a possible Dean, but that is not a question for quantification. When precision is required the criteria can be made so, and then, for instance

(20) Seven possible Deans are present

might be true. If we assume that a noun is a predicate and that a possible α is something which is possibly an α then the form of (20) is

(21) $\exists x(M\alpha \ \& \ \beta)$

Now it may be the case that, in the most usual sense of the phrase 'possible Dean', a possible Dean is someone who, although not perhaps a Dean, is nevertheless an actual person. But even if this were not so the predicate 'is present' certainly is existence-entailing and so (21) cannot be true unless there is an existing person who is a possible Dean and who is present. If we regiment Quine's example (Quine 1948, on p. 4 of Quine 1953) about the possible fat man in the doorway in the manner of (21) we get

(22) $\exists x(M(\textbf{\textit{fatman }} x) \ \& (\textbf{\textit{in the doorway }} x))$

Now **in the doorway** is an existence-entailing predicate if anything is and so (22) will be true iff there is something in the doorway of whom it is possible that it be a fat man. Again there may be questions about what kinds of things would qualify as being possibly fat men. If we suppose that the only things which could be men are humans, but that it is possible that any particular human be fat, then (22) will be true iff there is a person in the doorway, and so it has precise truth conditions. As will any extension of (22) to a sentence which answers the question 'how many possible fat men are in the doorway?'

I think what misled Quine was the thought that it had to be easier for a merely possible man to be in a doorway than for an actual man. Rather as if a merely possible man is an actual man who is very very thin and probably invisible as well. Perhaps such a man could actually be in the

57

doorway, but even in that case my guess is that there isn't one. You see (22) does not put the predicate ***in the doorway*** inside the scope of a modal operator, and that is why it is simply the assertion that of the things which are actually in the doorway, one of *them* is such that it is possible for it to be a fat man.

We can of course put both predicates inside the scope of a modal operator if we interpret the sentence to mean simply that it is possible for there to be a fat man in the doorway.

(23) $M\exists x((\textit{fatman } x) \ \& \ (\textit{in the doorway } x))$

and while that sentence may trouble those who dislike modality, it is not a problem about possibilist quantification.

Transmundism then allows possibilist quantification. That doesn't of course mean that it prohibits actualist quantifiers. Like David Lewis I conceive most natural-language quantifiers to be restricted in some way. In fact all of them are linguistically restricted by a noun, and in many cases extra restrictions are imposed by the context. If I say

(24) Everyone is present

it is little use objecting that the Queen is not here, if there was no reason to suppose that she should be.

Now where β is a predicate which is existence-entailing, and α is a noun which is not existence-entailing

(25) Every α is β

will be logically false unless α is restricted to actual α's. So, since context must be able to restrict quantifiers anyway, we may suppose that every α is intended to mean every actual α. We could reasonably postulate the existence of a conversational maxim to the effect that (25) is to implicate that the quantifier is to be restricted to those α's who are not conversationally ruled out as being β's.

5

Transmundism

In this chapter I want to take up some issues in the metaphysics of possible worlds. Although not strictly connected with the main theme of this book, it might help to get clear just what kind of metaphysical framework I am assuming, particularly since not all possible-worlds theorists adopt the same views. The view I shall be outlining is the one I called *transmundism* on page 43 and briefly outlined there. The first question I want to discuss is what Kaplan 1975 calls *haecceitism* and I want to see what this doctrine amounts to in a transmundist framework. Kaplan (Loux 1979, p. 217) defines haecceitism as the view that the same thing can exist in different possible worlds, and that a common 'thisness' may underlie extreme dissimilarity and distinct thisnesses may underlie great resemblance. Now the first feature of transmundism is that things *as such* are not located in worlds. For some entities, as discussed on pages 45–8, there is to be sure a property ω_{actual} such that a can be said to exist in world w iff $w \in \omega_{actual}(a)$. But ω_{actual} just happens to be one property among many, and it is no more metaphysically privileged, in a transmundist framework, than any other property. So the question of whether or not individuals can exist in more than one world turns out not to be a metaphysical question at all, but simply a question of whether the property ω_{actual}, that we express by using the word 'exists', allows there to be $w \neq w'$ such that $w \in \omega_{actual}(a)$ and $w' \in \omega_{actual}(a)$. I don't mean to claim that the question turns out to be simply a linguistic question. The issue is not about the English word 'exists'. It is about whether human beings in their communicative and conceptual activity have need of a property like ω_{actual} and whether, when they do, it ever allows $w \in \omega_{actual}(a)$ and $w' \in \omega_{actual}(a)$ for $w \neq w'$.

On page 46 I suggested that ω_{actual} is to be understood in terms of spatial location, and so it might seem that this could answer our question. Suppose for the present that all worlds have the same time scale and the same space. Certainly if a concrete object of ordinary discourse is appropriately modelled by a function *f* from worlds to sets of points $\langle p,m \rangle$ such that $\langle p,m \rangle \in f(w)$ is to mean that point *p* is one of the places at which *f* is located at moment *m* in world *w*, and if ω_{actual} is the function such that $w \in \omega_{actual}(f)$ iff $f(w) \neq \emptyset$ then indeed *f* can exist in more than one world. But that only pushes the problem back to whether functions like *f* are the appropriate models for the ordinary things we want to talk about, and once more turns the question from a metaphysical question into a question about which entities are important to us.

And even if we reject the analysis of individuals in terms of functions the existence property will still be defined in terms of a three-place ω such that $w \in \omega(a,p,m)$ iff in world *w* *p* is one of the points of space occupied by *a* at moment *m*. Now there will certainly be many *w* such that $w \in \omega(a,p,m)$ and $w' \in \omega(a,p',m')$ for $w \neq w'$. But the problem will be whether any of these ω's are candidates for a location property of a kind which might be used in ordinary discourse, and we are back at the question of what things speakers of a natural language conceive themselves to be talking about. If anti-haecceitism is the view that for metaphysical reasons you cannot have an existence predicate which allows things to exist in more than one world then transmundism is haecceitist. But transmundism is compatible with the view that the existence predicate of ordinary language does not permit transworld individuals.

Another way of formulating the question of haecceitism is as the doctrine that there are individual essences. Again transmundism can provide these in that there exists, for any *a*, a function ω_a such that for $b \in$ D and $w \in W$, $w \in \omega_a(b)$ iff $b = a$. This provides an essence which is not existence-entailing. There is also the function $\omega_a\star$ such that $w \in \omega_a\star(b)$ iff $w \in \omega_{actual}(a)$ and $a = b$. Again the issue is not a metaphysical one, but rather an issue about whether such functions are or are not accessible to speakers.

There is a third way of expressing the issue of haecceitism, and this way further supports the idea that the question of transworld identity, in a transmundist framework, is epistemological rather than metaphysical. It might be held that haecceitism is the view that there might be two worlds $w \neq w'$ such that the only difference between them is that two individuals *a* and *b* are interchanged. As a metaphysical view this is something which transmundism doesn't even allow you to state. It cannot be the view that all the properties *a* has in *w*, *b* has in *w'* and vice versa, since transmundism allows the property of being *a* and the property of being *b*. Certainly there will be properties ω which have the feature that for this particular w and w', $w \in \omega(a)$ iff $w' \in \omega(b)$, and for any $c \neq a$ and $c \neq b$, $w \in \omega(c)$ iff $w' \in \omega(c)$, and with respect to *these* properties w and w' cannot be distinguished. But the trouble is that such a class of properties can be defined for any $w \neq w'$. As an epistemological issue the matter is quite simple. For if the relevant class of properties includes all those that human beings have epistemological access to, then, while w and w' are metaphysically distinct worlds, no one can tell them apart. (It is of course the epistemological issue which Chisholm's Adam/Noah tale in Loux 1979 addresses.)

It isn't surprising that transworld identity is an epistemological matter. Consider Kripke's attempt to make the issue go away. (See Kripke 1972a, p. 267.) We *stipulate* that we have in mind a world in which *Humphrey* won the election. But if a hearer is to grasp our meaning the hearer must be able to tell whether or not a world is one of those. And that requires having the ability to tell whether a world *is* one of the stipulated ones, in which it is really Humphrey who has won, or whether it is a world in which only a look-alike has won. But if the properties epistemologically available to the hearer do not allow the difference to be recognized then no amount of stipulation can guarantee that the hearer gets hold of the right set of worlds. (It might even affect the content of the stipulation to begin with, for if the speaker can have no epistemological access to the difference it might be argued that the speaker cannot stipulate a content which is sensitive to the difference.)

According to transmundism, individuals as such are not located in worlds. Existence is one property among many, and it is properties that things, or n-tuples of things, have or lack at worlds. Similarly things *as such* cannot be said to be possible or impossible. This is important because one occasionally finds the following objection to possible-worlds theories: if you are going to allow things which are merely possible as well as things which are actual why stop there? Why not admit impossible things as well (Lycan: 1979, p. 313)? And that is absurd, so why not stop at the actual things? The mistake in this reasoning from a transmundist viewpoint is the supposition that things can be classified into the actual, the possible and the impossible. It is propositions, and so derivatively properties, which are so classified. A proposition p is (actually) true at w iff $w \in p$, it is (logically) possible iff $p \neq \emptyset$ and is (logically) impossible iff $p = \emptyset$. (The word 'actual' does have a more subtle role in natural language, in ways not presently relevant. See chapter 3 of Cresswell 1990.) Now the object usually chosen as an impossible object is Meinong's round square, and it is thought that a possible-worlds theorist ought to admit this as an object, albeit an impossible one. But in a transmundist model, the sentence 'the round square is impossible' would not be analysed as:

(1) $\exists x(round(x) \ \& \ square(x) \ \& \ impossible(x))$

but as

(2) $\sim M\exists x(round(x) \ \& \ square(x))$

It is not that there exists an object that is impossible, it is that the *properties* round and square are nowhere jointly exemplified because whatever precisely the functions ω and ω′ are which represent **round** and **square** they have the feature that for every *a*, ω(*a*) ∩ ω′(*a*) = ∅.

The critic of possible worlds will not be satisfied. Like Russell 1905 such a person will claim that if *that* is the argument against possible-worlds semantics then surely one can use a version of it against non-actual possibilia. The mistake in moving from (2) to (1) would be paralleled by the mistake in moving from

(3) $\sim \exists x \ King \ of \ France(x)$

to

(4) $\exists x(King \ of \ France(x) \ \& \ \sim Ax)$

I agree that this would be a mistake. For, just as a possible fat man who is actually in a doorway must exist so, since presumably **King of France** is an existence-entailing predicate (4) is logically false, since the first conjunct entails that *x* is actual.

The argument for possible individuals however goes like this. Assume at least one predicate which is not existence-entailing. That is, assume at least one predicate with free *x* such that α is true and *Ax* false. Then $\exists x(\alpha \ \& \sim Ax)$ is true and so $\exists$ must range over things which do not satisfy the existence predicate *A*. Now there *is* a parallel argument for impossibilia in the following way. Suppose that a predicate α is *strongly* non-existence-entailing iff there is some *x* such that α is true of it but, where *M* means the same as *possibly* on pages 27, 78 and 83, *MAx* is not. That is, $\exists x(\alpha \ \& \sim MAx)$ is true. Then $\exists$ must range over things which cannot possibly exist. What sorts of things these might be will depend on just what *A* amounts to. Suppose that 'exists' means 'has a spatial location'. Then, presumably, the empty set ∅ does not, in this sense, exist in any world. So, according to *this* definition the empty set will be an impossible object. If that is what is meant by admitting impossibilia then transmundism does allow them, but this has no metaphysical significance, since the existence predicate is not metaphysically privileged, and any predicate α can be prefixed by a possibility operator M to give the predicate $M\alpha$ of being possibly α. None of this is connected with the impossibility of the round square, for that impossibility concerns the specification of the object in the first place, not the attribution of some particular ontological status to a previously given object.

I want now to look at two views of possible worlds which, in different ways, might seem to challenge transmundism. One is Plantinga's version of actualism, and one is David Lewis's counterpart-theoretic modal realism. They are both views which admit possible worlds, but Plantinga doesn't allow non-existent objects and Lewis doesn't allow transworld identities. I have chosen them because they do assume possible worlds – and I am not at the moment concerned with those who have no use for worlds at all – and they are fairly explicit about the questions I am concerned with. Hopefully, what I say about them will carry over to many other views.

Plantinga is concerned to distance himself from what he calls the 'canonical conception' of possible worlds. The canonical conception is almost transmundism except for one crucial point. And that is that the quantifiers are always interpreted actualistically, in the sense that $\exists x\alpha$ is true in w iff α is satisfied in w by something which exists in w. The first part of Plantinga 1976 aims to shew that, despite this, the canonical conception is committed to non-existent objects. I agree with him on this, and that is why transmundism quantifies over them. Plantinga never *argues* that there is anything wrong with non-existent objects. His first paragraph speaks of 'the dubious notion that there are or could have been things that do not exist'. Later he says that this notion 'exacts a substantial ontological toll', and refers to it as a price that we should try to avoid paying if we can. Presumably Plantinga thought that adherents of the canonical conception supposed that they could avoid commitment to non-existent objects, and wished to avoid such commitment. Transmundists however accept such commitment from the outset and so Plantinga has no argument against them. And when we look at some of the troubles that Plantinga reveals as in store for the canonicalists we can see that they all result from the view that in any world you can only quantify over what exists in that world. Thus, one reason why Plantinga is not willing to analyse a property as a function from individuals to sets of worlds (or from worlds to sets of individuals) is that he claims that the set would not exist in worlds in which members of its extension do not exist. This may bother the canonicalist, who may therefore be unable to quantify over this entity, but it does not bother the transmundist, for whom existence has no metaphysical significance. Plantinga also objects to the canonical conception of property on the ground that it makes necessarily co-extensive properties identical. That objection would still apply to transmundism, but that is another issue, and I have set out at length in Cresswell 1985a why I don't believe that treating properties, propositions or what have you as finer-grained entities solves the problem of propositional attitudes (or any other problem).

Transmundism makes a distinction between what exists and what the quantifiers range over. But the point is not about the *word* 'exists'. In discussing the 'existence' property, I indexed it by the word 'actual' - and it would have been possible to retain the view that what exists is indeed what the quantifiers range over, but that not everything which exists is actual. Now Plantinga's positive account of the phenomena which lead transmundists to quantify over non-actuals is based on just such a distinction. Instead of individuals he speaks of individual essences. Individual essences *exist* in every world but are only *exemplified* in some worlds. The essence of Socrates is the property that Socrates, and only Socrates, has in every world in which he exists, and for the essence to be exemplified is for Socrates to exist. Plantinga doesn't identify this with any set-theoretical construction involving sets containing Socrates, since according to him such sets do not exist in worlds in which Socrates does not *exist*, and so are not available for quantification. So he has to introduce a parallel system of entities for which one can make the distinction that transmundism makes by marking off existence/ actuality from the domain of quantification. It should be clear that if α is a sentence of a language interpreted in a transmundist framework there is an equivalent Plantinga interpretation obtained by replacing every individual by its corresponding essence and every property of an individual by the corresponding property of its individual essence. If you think that this is an ontological advance then you are welcome to do this. In similar vein an objector to possible worlds may say, 'I don't believe in possible worlds but I do believe that for any set W of them there is an ordinal κ of the same cardinality as W and so I shall replace every $w \in W$ by some $\lambda_w \in \kappa$ and replace every property by the corresponding function from individuals to subsets of κ.' No transmundist will be impressed by this ontological 'reduction' or will be concerned to challenge it.

My second example of an apparent alternative to transmundism is David Lewis's version of modal realism. However, the issue is not the metaphysical one of whether possible worlds are to be taken realistically. Transmundism as such has nothing to say about where the members of W come from. They might be manufactured out of basic particular situations, as I once suggested, or they might be taken as primitive entities in their own right, or whatever. The feature of Lewis's metaphysics is that no individual exists in more than one world. The difference between Lewis's realism and transmundism is that for him it is a basic metaphysical fact that no individual can appear in more than one world, whereas for transmundism individuals as such do not appear in worlds; rather they have properties in worlds. Among these properties will be ω_{actual} but ω_{actual} is not metaphysically privileged.

Lewis (1986a, p. 50) defines a property as a set. The usual objection to doing so is that two distinct properties may determine the same set. Lewis points out that this is only an objection if you restrict yourself to things from the same world. Nothing prevents two distinct properties coinciding on the individuals from some particular world if they differ on individuals from another world. The problem is to find the appropriate way to compare Lewis's notion of property with a transmundist notion. On a transmundist account a property is something that an individual can have in one world and lack in another. Lewis says that that is not a property but a relation, so it seems that his notion of property is different from a transmundist's. Perhaps the only way to compare the notions is to look at what properties do in a transmundist framework, and see how Lewis would arrange for the same job to be done. Suppose that F is a one-place predicate and u is a logically proper name. Then if Fu is a subject–predicate sentence and V is a function in a transmundist framework which assigns a property to F and a member of D to u, we may define $V(Fu)$ to be $V(F)(V(u))$. Write $V(u)$ as $\bar{u}$ and $V(F)$ as ω and then $w \in V(Fu)$ iff $w \in \omega(\bar{u})$.

For Lewis the matter is not so straightforward. This is because $\tilde{u}$ will be taken from just a single world, and if $\omega^\star$ is any property then $\tilde{u} \in \omega^\star$ or $\tilde{u} \notin \omega^\star$ has an absolute truth value and this would make Fu non-contingent. Lewis of course agrees that a sentence like Fu can sometimes be contingent, and this is where he invokes the doctrine of counterpart theory. Although an individual cannot appear in more than one world yet it may have counterparts in other worlds. If you exist in world w and $w \neq w'$ then *you* cannot satisfy F in w but your counterpart might, so 'by courtesy' it will be said to be true that you are F in w because your w-counterpart is in the set assigned to F.

A transmundist may perhaps be less clear than some about whether counterpart theory really is a metaphysically different alternative. First, take a restricted version of counterpart theory whereby for any a and any w there is at most one b in w such that b is the w counterpart of a. We can refer to this as a_w. Now suppose that the counterpart relation is an equivalence relation, so that $(a_w)_{w'} = a_{w'}$ and that if a is in w then for any w' $(a_{w'})_w = a$. These are stronger conditions than Lewis requires, and abandoning them does indeed shew that counterpart theory gives different results from a straightforward transmundist theory. For Lewis we would have to say that $w \in V(Fu)$ iff the counterpart of $\bar{u}$ in w is a member of the set assigned to F. So given a set θ of Lewis-individuals, say that ω_θ is the transmundist property corresponding to θ iff for any individual a and $w \in W$: $w \in \omega_\theta(a)$ iff $a_w \in \theta$, where a_w is the counterpart of a in w, and we are assuming that a has at most one counterpart in each world. (If a has no counterpart in w then let $w \notin \omega_\theta(a)$.) According to this definition ω_D will be the property such that $w \in \omega_D(a)$ iff $a_w \in D$. And of course provided that a *does* have a counterpart in w then it will be in D and so $\omega_D(a)$ is just the set of worlds in which a has counterparts, which is what, for Lewis, the claim that a exists would amount to. Notice that counterpart theory allows the sentence that $\bar{a}$ exists to be true in more than one world even though metaphysically all individuals are world-bound. So it is still not clear that a Lewis metaphysics cannot be expressed in a transmundist framework.

However it seems that every property is existence-entailing. The reason is this. If $w \in \omega_\theta(a)$ then $a_w \in \theta$. But if $a_w \in \theta$ then $a_w \in D$ and so $w \in \omega_D(a)$, which is just how we say that a exists in w. Is there any way by which we may allow an ω_θ such that $w \in \omega_\theta(a)$ but a does not exist in w? The reply in the spirit of transmundism is this: our proof that Lewis cannot have a predicate which is not existence entailing depended on the assumption that both the counterpart relation and the existence-property are metaphysical notions. But why not say that the counterpart relation is wider than existence? That is, the mere fact that $a_w \in D$ is not sufficient to guarantee that a_w *exists* in w. So let us require that a has a counterpart in every world, but only some of the things which appear in that world may properly be said to *exist* in it. The things which appear in a given world are the things available in that world for picking out, via counterparts, things which genuinely exist in other worlds whether or not they exist in that world. This makes them a little like Plantinga's individual essences. Since ω_{actual} need no longer be ω_D we cannot argue that if $w \in \omega_\theta(a)$ then $w \in \omega_{actual}(a)$.

In the discussion so far I have assumed that the counterpart relation is an equivalence relation which picks out at most one thing in each world. If this is so then it is not hard to shew that counterpart theory is trivial. This is because for *any* three worlds (identical or distinct) w_1, w_2 and w_3, $w_1 \in \omega_\theta(a_{w2})$ iff $w_1 \in \omega_\theta(a_{w3})$. In other words, whether the property holds is completely unaffected by which individual is chosen. This fact gives the transmundist an innocuous way to interpret counterpart theory. For the transmundist can say that a_w is no more than a metaphorical way of talking about a-as-it-appears in w. The temporal parallel might be useful here. Suppose the question is how tall I was in 1952. What is important is that you won't get an answer to that question by measuring me in 1990. You can say if you like that the person you must measure is the me-in-1952 not the me-in-1990, but whether you want to talk this way or not has little significance for the way in which you are to establish that the property holds.

The matter does have some significance though if the counterpart relation does not yield a unique counterpart in each world. This can happen in two ways. One way is to imagine that for any a in world w_1 it is a matter to be determined by context just which b in w_2 is its counterpart. This amounts to saying that in different contexts different counterpart relations are involved. Lewis (1971) has suggested that although persons and bodies are identical, this is not a necessary truth because an a in w_1 may have a person-counterpart b in w_2 and a body-counterpart c in w_2 with $b \neq c$. In Cresswell 1990, pp. 178–87, I suggested a way of dealing with this whereby the members of D are functions whose values are the things Lewis calls ordinary individuals. That is one way of dealing with the matter since different counterpart relations make different functions and nothing is to stop $f(w_1) = g(w_1)$ and $f \neq g$ since $f(w_2) \neq g(w_2)$. But it isn't the only way of dealing with it. Recall that although a property for Lewis is just a set θ of individuals the use he makes of property-ascribing sentences requires us to make the transmundist property ω which corresponds to θ depend on the counterpart relation in question. Put formally this means that, where c is a particular counterpart relation, then $\omega_{(\theta, c)}$ can be defined to be the transmundist property such that $w \in \omega_{(\theta,c)}(a)$ iff $a_w \in \theta$ where a_w is the *c*-counterpart of *a* in *w*.

The more serious difference is where, according to the same counterpart relation, a single thing in one world may have more than one counterpart in another. This difference cannot be reflected in Lewis's notion of property but it does enter into his definition of the satisfaction conditions of the modal operators. In world *w* the sentence 'necessarily *u* is F' is true iff in every accessible world *all* of *u*'s counterparts are F, while 'possibly *u* is F' is true iff in some accessible world at least one is. Now there is nothing to prevent the introduction of a necessity operator which means that in all worlds at least one of *u*'s counterparts is F, or a possibility operator which means that in at least one world all of *u*'s counterparts are F. In fact the 'I might have been twins' motivation for double counterparts is surely a case where just that happens, at least if we don't adopt the suggestion in Cresswell 1990, p. 186, that in these cases the counterpart is a plural object. In a transmundist framework necessity is unambiguously an operation from sets of worlds to sets of worlds whereby $w \in \omega_{nec}(a)$ iff $w' \in a$ for every w' accessible from *w*; and possibility is its dual. Nevertheless, we can get the effect of Lewis's two kinds of necessity and two kinds of possibility if for each θ we define ω_θ^+ and ω_θ^-. $w \in \omega_\theta^+(a)$ iff for every counterpart *b* of *a* in *w*, $b \in \theta$, and $w \in \omega_\theta(a)^-$ iff there is some counterpart *b* of *a* in *w* such that $b \in \theta$. This is not to say there won't be *linguistic* considerations which distinguish the cases, since the question concerns the ambiguity or otherwise of the modal operator. But both ω_θ^+ and ω_θ^- are properties in a perfectly good transmundist sense.

One might therefore say that transmundism is only counterpart theory in fancy dress. That wouldn't worry a transmundist since the spirit of transmundism is that it is a mistake to put into the metaphysics differences which more properly hinge on epistemological and linguistic questions about which of the many entities that the metaphysics allows are important to us. I don't wish to dispute the importance of these other questions. Indeed transmundism is the view that it is these *non-*metaphysical questions which are the real ones, and transmundism itself is no more than a framework within which they can be raised.

Lewis also argues against haecceitism. One of the problems for transmundism is that according to it haecceitism does not seem even to be a statable position. The way Lewis states it is as follows. We distinguish among all the properties - which for Lewis are just sets of (world-bound) individuals – those which we can call *natural* properties. Lewis appears to take it to be a metaphysical matter just which properties are natural, though a transmundist will say that it is rather a question of which properties are important to us. Haecceitism is that it is possible for two worlds w_1 and w_2 to be distinct even though for every *natural* property θ, and any a in w_1, $a \in \theta$ iff $a_{w_2} \in \theta$. Lewis does not put the position as formally as that, but that can be the only way of making sense of it. When w_1 and w_2 are related like that it would seem plausible to suppose that every a in w_1 has a unique counterpart a_{w_2} in w_2, and that $(a_{w_2})_{w_1} = a$, even if this requirement does not hold in general. For transmundism this is very similar to the question of verificationism, since, if the natural properties are those that we have epistemological access to, then the question is whether two worlds may differ in ways that we are in principle unable to discern. The main problem with it is that it is presumably an empirical matter which properties are natural and so anti-haecceitism, as thus defined, sets logical limits on what we can in principle have epistemological access to. I am unclear how important an objection this is. It is one which is frequently made against combinatorialist accounts of possible worlds, since it is said that they circumscribe what is logically possible by limits which are too narrow. One reply is that since possible worlds are introduced as theoretical entities in the semantics of natural language they only need to generate as many possibilities as that language requires. Since the language is used by speakers in a particular world then, although they speak a language which allows them the possibility of referring to worlds which can be very unlike the world we are in, yet the nature of our world places some constraints on what other kinds of world there are. Be all that as it may, the question for transmundism is simply whether there are enough *natural* properties to determine uniquely each possible world. And whatever kind of question it is it is not a metaphysical one, and so transmundism does not have to take sides on it.

Transmundism is not just a particular metaphysical position. It also embodies a certain attitude to metaphysics, and I shall conclude by indicating what this attitude to metaphysics would look like in a quite different area. It is known that the axiom of choice is independent of the other axioms of set theory. If we call these ZF (though I personally prefer a set theory whose variables range over classes as well as sets) then both ZF + choice and ZF + the negation of choice are consistent if ZF itself is consistent. Faced with this fact, mathematicians are sometimes tempted to ask: but is choice *true*? Some think that there is a definite answer, some remain agnostic, while others say that the independence proofs shew that the concept of truth is not appropriate.

The equivalent of a transmundist in this area will say that none of these views is right. A transmundist will say that what the independence proofs shew is that there are at least two types of set-like objects. I'll call them presets. All presets satisfy ZF. A-type presets satisfy choice, while B-type presets satisfy the negation of choice. The independence proofs shew that if there are presets at all then there are both A-type and B-type presets. Is the axiom of choice true? Yes, if it's about A-type presets. No, if it's about B-type ones. But is it true about just plain *sets*? If there is to be an answer to this question it can only be found by saying to the mathematician: well, when you talk about sets, do you mean to be talking about A-type sets or about B-type sets? The choice (forgive the pun) is yours. Both are there. I don't mean to suggest it is up to each mathematician to stipulate which kind of preset is intended. But I do want to suggest that it is a matter of linguistic usage, and that, if any answer is not available, it is because the usage is indeterminate, not because the metaphysical facts are unknown.

The price of this solution is of course a bloated ontology. The transmundist welcomes a bloated ontology. This is because a transmundist feels that denying Ockham's razor is a small price to pay for a metaphysical principle which has gone almost completely unnoticed, which pulls in the opposite direction. That is the principle that a metaphysical system should be no stronger than necessary. I'll call this the principle of metaphysical weakness. Look at how it works in the set-theory case. The more traditional Platonist will want a set-theoretical universe which only contains the entities that are required for mathematics. So Ockham's razor throws out the others. This gives the axiom of choice a determinate metaphysically grounded truth value. The principle of metaphysical weakness entails that if you can have a set-theoretical framework which does not force you to give a particular truth value to the axiom of choice then such a framework is to be preferred to one which does force you to give a particular truth value. It must of course be a system that enables you to give the axiom a truth value, but only because you can *decide* what the entities are which the axiom is to be taken as referring to. In order to have such weakness the metaphysical system needs many more entities than Ockham's razor will permit. The principle of metaphysical weakness seems to me to be a much more illuminating principle than Ockham's razor, and more importantly for those of us engaged in the semantical study of natural language, it seems to be the principle that natural language assumes. And in possible-worlds semantics it is the transmundist framework which, by removing the question of haecceitism and the question of existence and the question of whether we quantify over possibilia or only over actual existents from the metaphysical sphere, seems to me to fit best with the principle of metaphysical weakness.

6

Putnam's 'Meaning of "meaning"'

In this chapter I want to discuss whether the things said in Putnam 1975 affect the kind of possible-worlds semantics illustrated in the case of the very simple language $\mathscr{L}$ introduced on pages 5f. Since Putnam's principal target is the use of the intension/extension distinction in semantics, and since that distinction is one which can be defined in $\mathscr{L}$, at least in the case of predicates (see p. 29), it is important to see how Putnam's remarks affect what has so far been said. In the latter part of the paper (pp. 183-8) Putnam offers a critique of what he calls 'California semantics'. The semantics I offered for $\mathscr{L}$ is clearly within this tradition. This section of Putnam's paper is, however, less helpful than other parts. Putnam's principal argument against California semantics is that treating an intension as a function from worlds to extensions requires supplementing by giving an account of what it is to 'grasp' an intension. The reason this is for him an important criticism is that the role of intension in semantics that he is concerned with is that it is the means by which a speaker is able to determine the extension, and treating it merely as a function from worlds to extensions gives no help in explaining how it can fill this role. I need take no issue with this criticism since I have already stressed that nothing in the possible-worlds semantics offered for $\mathscr{L}$ gives any help in saying what it is about speakers' behaviour that determines which of the many possible interpretations for $\mathscr{L}$ is the correct one. The real interest of Putnam's paper is whether the particular examples he gives earlier actually shew that an interpretation for $\mathscr{L}$ could not be the kind of $\langle W,D,V \rangle$ triple that it was defined to be on pages 18, 22 and 27 and in the Appendix on pages 32f.

Putnam's twin-earth example is so well known that it hardly needs repeating. Twin Earth is a planet just like Earth except that water on Twin Earth is not H_2O but has a chemical formula Putnam writes as XYZ. In 1750 chemists on Earth and Twin Earth did not know the chemical composition of the substances that they all called 'water'.

Putnam claims that when an Earthian speaker $Oscar_1$ uses the word 'water' he means H_2O, while his twin, $Oscar_2$, who may be an exact duplicate, and in exactly the same mental state as $Oscar_1$ will mean XYZ by *his* use of 'water'.

The moral Putnam draws from this is that '"meanings" just ain't the *head*'. Does this moral go against anything that we have said so far? Consider the status of the sentence

(1)   Water is H_2O.

One problem is that in 1750 the expression H_2O is not in the languages of Earth or Twin Earth. But we could imagine a time at which scientists on the two planets had the vocabulary but were only beginning to suspect what the composition of water was.

In order to see how this affects possible-worlds semantics we must follow Putnam and change the example slightly. Instead of supposing Twin Earth to be a planet like Earth somewhere else in the actual world, we suppose another possible world just like ours except that its Earth is like Twin Earth in that what is called 'water' there is XYZ and not H_2O. Call the actual world w_1 and its twin w_2. If, as argued in Cresswell 1978, knowing the meaning of (1) is knowing the conditions under which it is true then we have to look at its truth value in w_1 and w_2. Clearly it is true in w_1, but what of w_2? This depends on the meaning of 'water' and Putnam offers us a choice. First one might hold that 'water' is world-relative but constant in meaning, so that in w_2 water is XYZ. Second one might hold that water is H_2O in all worlds but that 'water' doesn't have the same meaning for speakers in w_1 and w_2. Putnam claims that the first view must be wrong. This is because he claims that what the original example established (where Earth and Twin Earth are in the same possible world) was that $Oscar_1$ and $Oscar_2$ mean something different by 'water'. $Oscar_1$ means H_2O and $Oscar_2$ means XYZ. The idea is that each Oscar can point to something and say

(2)   By 'water' I mean the stuff that is the same liquid as *that*.

Putnam symbolizes the 'same liquid' relation as $same_L$. I regard it as relatively uncontentious that the stuff which is in fact water has its essential features in terms of its chemical composition, so that the stuff which is in fact H_2O is that in all possible worlds in which it exists. But this uncontentious fact doesn't alone help in establishing the meaning of 'water'. For even on Putnam's first alternative the stuff which is water in

w_1 would still be H_2O in w_2. It's just that it would no longer be *water*. Just as the fact that it is essential to a bachelor to be human means that he would still be human even in a world in which he is no longer a bachelor. Nevertheless, there is some plausibility that (2) does represent how the word 'water' is used, and if it does then Putnam's second way seems correct.

If we adopt this then, for a speaker of English in w_1, (1) is true in all possible worlds, while for a speaker of English in w_2 (we could call it twin English) (1) is false in all possible worlds. If English and twin English share the same syntax the difference would be that the intended interpretation for English might be a triple $\langle W,D,V_1\rangle$ while that for twin English might be $\langle W,D,V_2\rangle$. Then

(3) $V_1(1) = W$

while

(4) $V_2(1) = \emptyset$

And here is the problem because in 1750 nobody knew that (1) is true. So it seems that in 1750 people were ignorant of a necessary truth. At least that is so if in 1750 the people who used (1) could be said to know its meaning. One way of making Putnam's claims compatible with the claims of Cresswell 1978 is to say that there is a sense in which English speakers *didn't know* what (1) meant. If we say this we must surely allow that there is another sense in which they did know. It is here that Putnam's positive thesis comes in. What Putnam does is set out a number of tests which must be passed by a speaker to count as mastery of the word in question. These involve being able to recognize stereotypical cases, and I will not have anything to say about them here except to observe that they do not involve knowing the intension, in the sense of intension relevant to possible–worlds semantics. Given that speakers can use a word without knowing its meaning (in at least one sense of knowing its meaning) there is no problem about (1).

Putnam's example used natural-kind terms and this certainly takes us beyond the resources of $\mathscr{L}$. However Putnam is convinced that his problem is very widespread and I shall try to see how close you can get in $\mathscr{L}$. One of the symbols of $\mathscr{L}$ is **whistles**, and if $\langle W,D,V_1\rangle$ is the intended interpretation to $\mathscr{L}$ then

74

(5) $V_1(\textbf{\textit{whistles}})$ is a function ω such that for any $a \in D$ and any $w \in W$, $w \in \omega(a)$
      iff a whistles in w

Assume that w_1 is the real world. In the real world when someone
whistles a certain sound is produced as air flows through a certain sort of
aperture in the lips. Suppose that in w_2, unknown to the speakers of twin
English, this sound is produced by some completely different mechanism,
perhaps a certain sort of ray hits a sensitive spot in the 'hearer's' head,
which sets off a sound that can't be distinguished from a whistle. Now I
admit that I am not really confident about the individuation of activities
but one might make a case along Putnam's lines for saying that this isn't
whistling though it *is* what the w_2 speakers mean by **whistles**, and so in the
interpretation $\langle W,D,V_2 \rangle$ which reflects *their* use of $\mathscr{L}$,

(6) $V_2(\textbf{\textit{whistles}})$ is the function ω' such that for $a \in D$ and any $w \in W$, $w \in \omega'(a)$
      iff a does in w what it takes to produce in w_2 the effect that is
      indistinguishable from whistling in w_1.

This doesn't add anything new to the discussion but it does shew how
Putnam's observations could apply to a language as simple as $\mathscr{L}$.

If that were all there were to be said the problem would be a relatively
simple one. But it has depended on the claim that speakers of $\mathscr{L}$ in w_1
who don't recognize its truth have to be said, in some sense, not to know
its meaning. I believe that the 'in some sense' can be used to take much of
the sting out of the claim, especially if we have an account of standards for
mastery of a term. But it still leaves us with the problem of giving an
account of why it is that what seems like an empirical discovery by
chemists is really a discovery about the meaning of the term 'water'. In
some sense the answer is relatively straightforward. We imagined the use
of 'water' being determined ostensively in accordance with (2). In w_1 the
speaker is pointing to H_2O, while in w_2 the speaker is pointing to XYZ.
So one thing that the chemists could have discovered is that what
everyone had been pointing to was H_2O rather than XYZ. This could be
misleadingly described by saying that although it has turned out that
water is H_2O, it might have turned out that water was XYZ. Putnam on
p. 159 uses this expression in just this way to indicate a situation in which
XYZ rather than H_2O looks like water, tastes like water, fills the lakes
and so on. He follows Kripke in saying that although it is *metaphysically
necessary* that water is H_2O yet it is not *epistemically necessary*. This
terminology has become common. It seems to me that at best it labels the

problem while at worst it incorrectly claims that there are two kinds of necessity and that the same thing can be necessary in one sense but not necessary in another sense.

Notice what is being claimed when it is claimed that it might have turned out that water was XYZ. If it had so turned out then what everybody would then have been referring to as 'water' would not have been water but would have been XYZ. Imagine the following parody: English speakers in w_1 point to pigs and say

(7) By 'pig' I mean something which is the same animal as *that*.

In w_2 the same speakers point to *birds* and say (7). Now look at the sentence

(8) Pigs can fly.

Example (8) is of course false. But it might certainly have turned out that things English speakers call 'pigs' had been birds, indeed in w_2 it is so. So can we say (9)?

(9) It might have turned out that pigs could fly.

It seems clear to me that we cannot. And if we cannot then more must be said about the 'water' case. The more that must be said is that there is something about the word 'water' *even when it means* H_2O that allows, as epistemically possible, worlds in which water is XYZ, whereas the use of 'pigs' to refer to pigs does not allow, for the purpose of (9), an epistemically possible world in which 'pigs' refers to birds.

It may be that this is the problem that Putnam wants to solve using the notion of a stereotype. For the person uttering (2) in w_1 is supposed to have the same stereotype of 'water' as does the person uttering it in w_2. But presumably, the person uttering (7) in w_1 does not have the same stereotype as the person uttering it in w_2. Now this may satisfy Putnam but it is difficult to see how to get an adequate semantics for (9) out of it in a way that makes (9) false but

(10) It might have turned out that water was XYZ

true. In particular it is very difficult to see how a different sense of *possibility* is involved from the sense in which both

(11) Pigs might have been able to fly

and

(12) Water might have been XYZ

are false. And even if there is such a sense, it is difficult to see how the semantics of the verbal expression 'turn out' can mark this distinction. Surely the situation is that what is possible is different in each case. One is that water cannot be H_2O nor can pigs fly. In the (9)/(10) case it is that words might have been used differently. We could say that taken literally (9) and (10) are just as false as (11) and (12) but that we sometimes *use* (9) and (10) as an inaccurate way of saying something quite different. Presumably such an account claims that we do this because the ordinary speaker, in pointing to water, does not know the difference between H_2O and XYZ, though *does* know the difference between pigs and birds.

Suppose however that we still do think that the distinction is semantic, but suppose we agree that it is not a distinction between kinds of possibility but in what it is which is supposed to be possible. If so we ought to be able to express the distinction in a language like $\mathscr{L}$ or an extension of it. It would probably turn out in that case that (9) and (11), and also (10) and (12), will have both readings and that the purpose of the verb 'turn out' will be to indicate that the preferred reading is that of envisaging a change of meaning. So how can we express the meaning of the word 'water' so that it allows the relevant distinction? Before we do let us be quite clear what the current enterprise is. We first looked at the view that the word 'water' simply has two meanings. In the English used in w_1 it simply means H_2O. So (1) is necessarily true and (12) is false. (In the English spoken in w_2 of course (1) is necessarily false and (12) is true.) Strictly speaking (10) is also false. But we use a pragmatic principle of charity to allow us to use (10) to record the possibility that 'water' could have referred to XYZ. That explanation seemed defective since it seems part of the *meaning* of 'water' to allow (10) in a way in which the meaning of 'pigs' in w_1 does *not* allow (9). So we are now looking at how the meaning of the word 'water' could allow the truth of (10) but the falsity of (12).

If we treat 'water' simply as the name of a natural kind there seems no way, within possible-worlds semantics, to express the distinction. However we might make some progress if we recall that not all subject–predicate sentences are interpreted as predicates applying to names. Thus **nobody** is in category $(s/(s/n))$ in making a name out of a one-place predicate. So we could treat **water** as an expression in category $(s/(s/n))$. This means that $V_1(\textbf{water})$ will be a function whose arguments are themselves functions. In order to express the distinction between (10) and (11) we use the fact that an expression in category (s/(s/n)) can have wide or narrow *scope*. For those who have not come across this distinction before I shall illustrate it using the word **everyone**. Imagine a collection of people playing a game in which all of them have a chance of winning but in which there can only be one winner. Then consider the two sentences

(13) Everyone possibly wins
(14) Possibly everyone wins.

Example (13) is true, because each one has a chance of winning, but (14) is not because there can only be one winner. In (13) it appears that **possibly** modifies the predicate **wins** while in (14) it modifies the sentence

(15) **everyone wins**.

In order to preserve **possibly** as a single symbol in a categorial language it is customary to use a device known as λ-abstraction. The predicate expression **possibly wins** will be represented as

(16) (λx **possibly** x **wins**)

Read λx as 'is an x such that'. The semantics of λ-abstraction requires the use of a value assignment to the individual variables as introduced on page 00. Where v is such an assignment let $(v, a/x)$ be the assignment exactly like v except that $(v, a/x)(x) = a$. Then for any $a \in D$ and wff α, $V_v(\lambda x \alpha)$ is the function ω such that $\omega(a) = V_{(v, a/x)}(\alpha)$. In the case of (16) this means that where $\langle W, D, V \rangle$ is the 'right' interpretation for English then

(17) $V(16) = \omega^\star$, where $\omega^\star$ is the function such that for $a \in D$ and $w \in W$:
(18) $w \in \omega^\star(a)$ iff for some w' such that $w R w'$, a wins in w'

We can now express the two senses of (15)

(19) **everyone** (λx **possibly** x **wins**)
(20) **possibly everyone wins**

The meaning of **everyone** is a function whose arguments are themselves functions from things to sets of worlds. This is because **everyone** is in category (s/(s/n)) and makes a sentence out of a one-place predicate - either a simple predicate like **wins** or a complex predicate like (16). In the intended interpretation $\langle W, D, V \rangle$, V(**everyone**) is the function such that where ω is any function from individuals to sets of worlds and $w \in W$:

(21) $w \in V(everyone)(\omega)$ iff for every person $a \in D$, $w \in \omega(a)$.

With $V(16)$ as $\omega^\star$ then $V(21)$ gives us that $w \in V(19)$ iff for every person a there is a world w' such that wRw' and a wins in w'. And this is just the meaning that everyone has a chance to win. Example (19) does not claim that the world in which a wins is the same as the world in which some other b wins. To make that claim we need (20). Since $w \in V(\textit{wins})(a)$ iff a wins in w then (15) will be true iff for every person a, a wins in w. And then, by $V(\textit{possibly})$ on page 27, (20) will be true iff there exists a world w' such that wRw' and (15) is true in w'. And this does require a world in which everyone wins, and since we are assuming a game in which that cannot happen (20) is false though (19) is true.

So much is standard. The new feature is to apply this to water. If *water* is to be in category $(s/(s/n))$ its meaning must take as arguments functions from things to sets of worlds. If we follow Putnam we shall suppose that what would have turned out according to (10) is that the stuff that is called 'water' that people drink, that fills the lakes, etc. - in short the stuff that we shall say plays the *water role* - was XYZ and not H_2O. So we have

(22) $w \in V(\textit{water})(\omega)$ iff there exists a substance a which plays the water role in w and $w \in \omega(a)$.

Notice that I have not made a distinction between English and twin English. This is because on the present account we are trying to shew how 'water' can have a single meaning in both languages and still preserve the falsity of (12) in w_1. The falsity of (12), remember, is not just the fact that water *isn't* XYZ in w_1 - so it's not Putnam's first solution. It's that in w_1 water couldn't be XYZ - that water isn't XYZ in *any* world. I shall take the phrase 'is XYZ' to be a simple one-place predicate. I shall also assume that XYZ, like H_2O, applies to things whose chemical composition is part of their essential nature, so that if a is XYZ (or H_2O) in any world then a is XYZ (or H_2O) in every world in which it exists. We represent the difference between (10) and (12) by

(23) **possibly water is XYZ**

and

(24) **water** (λx **possibly** x **is XYZ**)

Where $V(\textit{is XYZ})$ is the function ω' such that for $a \in D$, $w \in \omega'(a)$ iff a's chemical constitution is XYZ (note that I have not said 'XYZ in w' since its chemical constitution is essential to a), (23) will be true in w iff for some w' such that wRw',

(25) **water is XYZ**

is true in w'. And this will be so iff

(26) $w' \in V(\textbf{water})(\omega')$

By (22), (26) will hold iff there is some a such that a plays the water role in w' and a's chemical constitution is XYZ. So provided $w_1 R w_2$ then, since (25) is true in w_2, (23) is true in w_1. But consider (24). The semantics for λ-abstraction gives us that

(27) $w \in V(\lambda x \text{ } \textbf{possibly } x \textbf{ is XYZ})(a)$

iff there exists a world w' such that $w R w'$ and a is XYZ. (Again notice that being XYZ is not a world-relative notion.) This means that (24) is true in w iff there exists $a \in D$ where a plays the water role in w and there exists a world w' such that $w R w'$ and a is XYZ. But since being XYZ is not world-relative this means that the truth of (24) in a world w entails that what plays the water role in w is XYZ. But in w_1 H_2O and not XYZ plays the water role and so (24) is false in w_1.

At this point someone might object that in making the *meaning* of water depend on playing the water role we are ignoring the possibility introduced in Kripke 1972b, p. 157, and quoted with approval by Putnam on page 152, of using a description to fix the reference of a term in such a way that the description is not part of the meaning of the term. This is because in the present case the description, 'that which plays the water role in our world', which may be regarded as a description of what is going on in (2), *has* become part of the meaning of the word 'water'. Agreed. That distinction has been ignored. It has been ignored because we supposed someone suggesting that the difference between the (10)/(12) case, the water case, and the (9)/(11) case, the pigs case, was because there was something about the *meaning* of the word 'water' - not just a fact about how that word was introduced - which permitted (10) to be true but did not permit (9) to be true.

It is not so clear unfortunately that the technique used for **water** will work for verbs. Suppose, as I suggested, that what plays the 'whistling role' in w_2 is a quite different activity from what plays that role in w_1. Further, suppose that the physiology of those in w_2 is such that they cannot whistle. What this means is that if $\langle W,D,V_1 \rangle$ is the right interpretation for the language spoken in w_1 then

(28) $w_2 \notin V_1(\textbf{possibly Adriane whistles})$

Since **Adriane** is a name there will be no difference between

(29) **possibly Adriane whistles**

and

(30) **Adriane** (λx **possibly** x **whistles**)

and in fact there doesn't seem any possibility of using scope in any remotely natural way to capture the sense of

(31) It might have turned out that Adriane whistles

in which a w_1 speaker, attempting to describe what is going on in w_2, wants to express the fact that although whistling - in the w_1 sense - is not anything an inhabitant of w_2 can perform yet there is a world possible relative to w_2 - in fact w_1 is one - in which what plays the whistling role is something that Adriane does perform. Even if whistling is not a good example I see no reason for supposing that verbs cannot be just as much subject to the twin-earth problem as nouns.

There is another way of achieving the distinction between (10) and (12). That is by making use of the distinction introduced in Kaplan 1979, p. 84 between content and character. 'I' has a character which is constant for all speakers. It is that function which associates with the utterance context of any sentence the utterer of that sentence. In each context the particular speaker is the 'content' of 'I'. Kaplan's point is that although the content of 'I' will change from context to context it will, for a given context, retain the same content however far it is embedded in the sentence. This may seem a little obscure so I will try to describe how it applies to Putnam's case. If you think about how the worlds w_1 and w_2 enter the picture you will see that they do so in two ways. First, each world determines the brand of English spoken, in the sense that, on at least one version of the story, **water** in w_1 *means* H_2O, while in w_2 it means XYZ. But given the meaning of **water** in w_1 there is the question of what to say about that stuff in w_2. And that stuff is still H_2O not XYZ. This suggests that we are *really* interested in what happens at a *pair* of worlds rather than at a single world. This mechanism is sometimes referred to as 'double indexing'. I have no objection to that name - after all there *are* two world indices involved - but there is another use of double indexing which might be a little different. I am referring to the use of multiple indexing in the study of the semantics of *actually* operators (see chapter 3 of Cresswell 1990). This use *may* be the same, and is probably related, but it is best for now to think of it as a different phenomenon.

Kaplan's original reason for introducing the character/content distinction may be illustrated by looking at what might be thought wrong about the sentence (25). If you look at the semantics given you will see that it is true in a world w iff whatever plays the water role in w is XYZ. But that makes (25), although still false in w_1, true in w_2. But (25) on Putnam's view is supposed to be a sentence which is a metaphysical impossibility. Since (25) does not have a ***possibly*** operator in it there is no way of using scope to get the right meaning. One reply is that the only reason for saying that (25), when uttered in w_1, should be impossible is that we are persuaded of the falsity in w_1 of (24) and we think that because (24) is false in w_1 then (25) should be impossible. But this, it might be said, is just like arguing that the negation of

(32) The present King of France is bald

ought to be false because

(33) The present King of France is not bald

is false. Since (24) is not formed by putting ***possibly*** in front of (25) there is no reason for (25) to be a necessary falsehood. In fact it was important that it is not so that (23) can be used to give the 'it might have turned out' sense.

A context can of course include information about many things: who is speaking, who is being spoken to, what time it is, and so on. For our purposes we are only interested in the context world, for we are interested in someone uttering (25) in w_1 or in w_2. If we use the model illustrated in (31) we will say that a sentence is true at a set of pairs, where the first world in the pair can be called the *evaluation* world, and the second the *context* world. If the semantic values of sentences are sets of world–world pairs then the values of one-place predicates will be functions from individuals to sets of world–world pairs. If ***water*** remains in category (s/(s/n)) and if $\langle W,D,V \rangle$ is now the intended interpretation for English using a double-indexed semantics, we have, for any function ω from individuals to sets of world–world pairs, and any world–world pair $\langle w,w' \rangle$

(34) $\langle w,w' \rangle \in V(\textbf{water})(\omega)$ iff there exists a substance a which plays the water role in w', and $\langle w,w' \rangle \in \omega(a)$.

In claiming that a sentence is metaphysically necessary in a context w' one is, on this view, claiming that it is true in $\langle w,w'\rangle$ for every $w \in W$, but keeping w' the same. Kaplan's idea of course is that this kind of necessity applies to the *content* of a sentence. *is XYZ* is, I take it, a predicate whose meaning does not depend on the utterance context. Thus

(35) $\langle w,w'\rangle \in V(\textbf{is XYZ})(a)$ iff a's chemical composition is XYZ.

So on this semantics

(36) $\langle w,w'\rangle \in V(25)$ iff there is a substance a which plays the water role in w' and a's chemical composition is XYZ.

So suppose that (25) is uttered in w_1. Then, by (36), since what plays the water role in w_1 does *not* have XYZ as its chemical composition, $\langle w,w'\rangle \notin V(25)$ no matter what w may be. So on this semantics (25) in context w_1 is true at no evaluation world. Now consider (23). The double-indexed semantics for (metaphysical) possibility works on the evaluation index.

(37) $\langle w,w'\rangle \in V(\textbf{possibly})(p)$ iff there exists w'' such that $w\text{R}w''$ and $\langle w'',w'\rangle \in p$.

Here p is the set of world–world pairs representing the proposition being modified. It should be clear that

(38) $\langle w_1,w_1\rangle \notin V(\textbf{possibly})(V(25))$

so (23) is false at $\langle w_1,w_1\rangle$.

Example (24) will also be false, and the question arises of how to give the sense in which (23) is true. One of Kaplan's claims was that the meaning of a word only worked on the content. In other words it only changes the evaluation index. To get the 'might have turned out' sense we have to use a device which changes the context world as well. What we need is what Stalnaker 1978 calls a †-operator. (In the use of double indexing to deal with 'actually' operators such an operator was called on page 37 of Cresswell 1990 a *Ref* operator.) What a † operator does is identify the reference world with the evaluation world. Where p is a set of world–world pairs then

(39) $\langle w,w'\rangle \in V(\dagger)(p)$ iff $\langle w,w\rangle \in p$.

We may regard the † as a signal that Kaplan's restriction that only the evaluation world is involved in the meaning of operators is being suspended at that point. We can then define the intended sense of (10) as:

(40) **possibly †*water is XYZ***

We work out the truth value of (40) in $\langle w_1, w_1 \rangle$ as follows.

$\langle w_1, w_1 \rangle \in V(40)$

iff for some w' such that $w_1 R w'$

(41) $\langle w', w_1 \rangle \in V(†$*water is XYZ*).

Assuming that $w_1 R w_2$ then it will be sufficient for the truth of (40) that

(42) $\langle w_2, w_1 \rangle \in V(†$*water is XYZ*)

But (42) will hold iff

(43) $\langle w_2, w_1 \rangle \in V(†)V(25)$

iff

(44) $\langle w_2, w_2 \rangle \in V(25)$

iff, by (36), there is a substance *a* which plays the water role in w_2 which is XYZ. Since XYZ does play the water role in w_2 this means that (40) is true in $\langle w_1, w_1 \rangle$.

This method will even work for the whistling case. The predicate ***whistles*** in a double-indexed semantics, unlike ***is XYZ***, *is* a context-dependent verb. For recall that the claim is that what plays the role of whistling in w_1 is something that people in w_2 cannot perform, though of course they *can* perform in w_2 the activity that plays the role of whistling in w_2. So

(45) $\langle w, w' \rangle \in V(\textbf{\textit{whistles}})(a)$

iff *a* performs in *w* the activity that plays the role of whistling in w'.

In discussing the whistling case we imagined (28) being uttered by a speaker in w_1. That means that we take the context world to be w_1 and the evaluation world to be w_2. This means that we are looking at the truth of (28) at $\langle w_2, w_1 \rangle$. This will hold iff for some *w* such that $w_2 R w$,

(46) $\langle w, w_1 \rangle \in V(\textbf{\textit{Adriane whistles}})$

and (46) will hold iff Adriane performs in *w* the activity that plays the role of whistling in w_1. But we have supposed that the physiology of people in w_2 means that they cannot perform this activity, and so there is no *w* such that $w_2 R w$ in which they do. To get the sense of (31) we use a † operator. The sentence is

(47) **possibly †*Adriane whistles***

Example (47) will be true at $\langle w_2, w_1 \rangle$ iff there exists a world w such that $w_2 R w$ and

(48) $\langle w, w_1 \rangle \in V(\text{†}\textbf{\textit{Adriane whistles}})$

iff

(49) $\langle w, w_1 \rangle \in V(\text{†})V(\textbf{\textit{Adriane whistles}})$

iff

(50) $\langle w, w \rangle \in V(\textbf{\textit{Adriane whistles}})$

iff Adriane in w performs the activity that plays the role of whistling in w. Since it is reasonable to suppose that there may be such a world there is nothing to stop (47) being true at $\langle w_2, w_1 \rangle$ despite Adriane's physiological inability to do in w_2 what counts as whistling in w_1.

Putnam details some views of his own about the nature of meaning on pages 190f. Unfortunately they are not in a form in which they could be incorporated into a formal semantical theory. An important element in Putnam's notion of meaning is that of a *stereotype*. Although a tiger need not be striped, having stripes is part of our stereotype of tiger and is one of the tests for mastery of the word 'tiger'. Knowing the appropriate biological constitution of tigers is not necessary for having mastery of the word. This seems odd to me. Suppose tigers on Twin Earth are not striped but that Twin Earth speakers use 'tiger' to refer to just the same animals as we do. Are we to say that 'tiger' on Twin Earth can't mean tiger even though we on Earth can say (51) truly?

(51) No Twin Earth tigers have stripes.

Meaning involves the stereotype in conjunction with what Putnam calls 'extension'. Actually he can't really mean extension since he describes the 'extension' of 'water' on page 191 as H_2O. But the extension of water in a particular world will be the particular totality of H_2O in that world. Since one can certainly say

(52) There might have been more water than there is

then what Putnam is calling extension is what in possible-worlds semantics would be intension. The intension, in this sense, of 'water' would take you from a world w to the totality of water in w. Is stereotype + intension sufficient to help with the problem of (10)? For (10) to be true we have to know that XYZ plays the water role in w_2. Can the stereotype do this? Suppose that XYZ in w_2, many years before 1750, before indeed there were any speakers of Twin English, was colourless, drinkable and so on. Suppose in short that it once *did* satisfy the w_1 water stereotype (though of course it wasn't *water* because it wasn't H_2O) but that it no longer does. Indeed it never was the stereotype of water for any Twin-Earth speakers of any Twin-Earth language. It seems to me that the existence of this XYZ means that (10) could be true, in whatever sense it was already supposed to be, even though neither the extension nor the stereotype are the same.

Nor does stereotype in conjunction with intension seem sufficient to deal with (10). For suppose that there is a small amount of H_2O in w_2, that it *does* satisfy the w_1 water stereotype but that it does not play the water role in w_2 - XYZ plays that role though XYZ doesn't satisfy the stereotype. Since H_2O does not play the water role in w_2 its presence there, even with its stereotype, cannot guarantee the truth of (10) in w_1. Of course if you build playing the water role into the account of what a stereotype is you will take care of these objections but then you will get precisely the kind of theory that, when formalized in possible-worlds semantics, will, as near as makes no difference, be a theory like the double-indexed semantics presented above. (A more elaborate account of a semantics which takes into account that words may have different meanings in different worlds may be found in Thomason 1976.)

Putnam's use of the twin-earth examples has been held to have disastrous consequences for the semantics of propositional attitudes. In chapter 3 of Schiffer 1987 Stephen Schiffer argues that belief cannot be a relation between people and propositions however these latter are construed provided that they are language-independent entities which have their truth conditions essentially. He considers (p. 51) that his arguments are not dependent on a particular view of propositions; so I shall consider propositions to be sets of possible worlds, properties to be functions from individuals to sets of worlds, (intensional) relations to be functions from n-tuples of individuals to sets of worlds, and so on. Schiffer's principal objection to belief as a relation between people and propositions is based on natural-kind words and his chief example is

(53) Tanya believes that Gustav is a dog.

I shall discuss later what Schiffer says about (53) but I shall begin by applying what I have already said in discussing Putnam to the case of belief. The discussion on pages 75–85 above did not involve the semantics of belief sentences but it is not too hard to see a connection between

(54) Oscar believes that water is H_2O

and

(55) It might have turned out that water was XYZ.

Presumably (54) is true because of a scientific and not a logical discovery. And Putnam makes it fairly clear that what the scientific discovery did was rule out certain worlds. Not, of course, worlds in which water is XYZ – there are none – but worlds in which XYZ plays the water role. So what Oscar believes is that what (55) says might have been so is not in fact so.

In discussing the 'might have turned out' example I approached it in two ways depending on whether a pragmatic or semantic explanation is given. On the pragmatic account (55) is just as false as

(56) Water might have been XYZ

(when these are uttered on Earth). However someone uttering (55) might be taken to be saying that the word 'water' might have been used differently by speakers who were not able to distinguish between H_2O and XYZ. On this account (55) as spoken on Earth literally means

(57) It might have turned out that H_2O was XYZ

and on this account (54) means the same as

(58) Oscar believes that H_2O is H_2O.

In some cases it does seem reasonable to think that the replacement of 'water' by 'H_2O' makes no difference.

(59) Oscar believes that water is wet

could mean the same as

(60) Oscar believes that H_2O is wet.

Of course the pragmatic account says more than that (59) and (60) *could* mean the same – it says that taken literally they always do. I mention this because the semantic accounts we looked at on pages 77–80 would allow both transparent and opaque readings for (59) and (60) and so would permit a sense of (59) in which it is equivalent to (60).

So what of Schiffer's arguments against propositions if we accept the pragmatic account? If the pragmatic account is accepted then the semantics will follow what Schiffer on page 54 calls the classical theory. His version of this is that the content of Tanya's belief, in sentence (53), is the pair

(61) ⟨Gustav, Doghood⟩

where doghood is the property of being a dog. In possible-worlds semantics this is the function ω such that, for any a, ω(a) is the set of worlds in which a is a dog. (Alternatively it could be the function from worlds to 'extensions' which gives, for each world, the set of things which are dogs in that world.) On page 56 Schiffer poses the question 'Exactly what property is this property of being a dog?' At this point it is worth recalling a distinction made in chapter 5 of Montague 1974. Richard Montague, in analysing the ontological status of a number of philosophical entities, carefully distinguishes on page 152 between saying what the entity *is*, in terms of its ontological status, and giving a *definition* of just *which* entity it is. For instance, Montague takes events to be properties of times, but does not claim to say what property a particular event is. Montague correctly points out that doing the former need not require you to do the latter. Doghood is simply the function ω which takes any a into the set of worlds in which a is a dog. One reply to this is not open to Schiffer. He cannot say: 'I don't accept that there are such things as possible worlds or that properties are functions such as ω.' He cannot say this because he is explicitly claiming that his arguments do not depend on rejecting propositions (and therefore properties) because they are 'creatures of darkness' (p. 49) and ontologically dubious. He says that even granted they exist, belief cannot be a relation to them. So he must accept the existence of such an ω.

What then is he asking? Schiffer offers us two alternatives. Either we can give an account of doghood, or the property of being a dog cannot be specified in other terms. Schiffer first supposes that the property of being a dog can be specified in other terms. He follows Putnam in accepting that these other terms may be no more known to Tanya than H_2O is known to Oscar. Suppose that there is a natural kind, *Canis familiaris*, and that being a dog means being a member of that kind. If that is so, says Schiffer, then the content of Tanya's belief is 'now revealed to be'

(62) ⟨⟨Gustav, *Canis familiaris*⟩, the kind-membership relation⟩

There is an immediate problem here because (62) is clearly a different structure from (61), and on some accounts (62) would express the different belief that Gustav is a member of the kind *Canis familiaris*, a belief that it is supposed Tanya need not have. In supposing that ω can be analysed in terms of membership in a natural kind we are not supposing that the content of Tanya's belief is to be represented by (62). Rather we are supposing that the content is still (61), *viz.* the pair ⟨Gustav, ω⟩, but that the property ω (a function from individuals to sets of worlds) can be analysed by stipulating that for any world *w* and any individual *a*,

(63) $w \in \omega(a)$ iff *a* is a member (in *w*) of the kind *Canis familiaris*.

(In (63) I have put 'in *w*' in parentheses because membership of a natural kind may be an essential property, and hold of *a*, if at all, in every world in which *a* exists.)

Schiffer (p. 57) imagines us to come across creatures whom we mistakenly suppose not to be dogs but who are in fact members of *Canis familiaris*. We call them shmogs. Schiffer claims that

(64) Tanya believes that Gustav is a shmog

is false. Now it may be that (62) does not accurately report the content of Tanya's belief as reported in (64) but it is not clear that (61) does not, and if so then on the pragmatic account (64) is true because (53) is true. Of course this may shew that the pragmatic account is wrong but all I am doing here is to shew that if you accept it for the Putnam example then you are no worse off in Schiffer's example.

Suppose that ω cannot be specified in other terms. In such a case, Schiffer says on page 58, it would have to be 'primitive and irreducible'. This of course means no more than that you cannot specify it in other terms, where presumably these other terms are the primitives of your favourite theory. But Schiffer takes it to mean more. He takes it that if ω is primitive and irreducible then it would be logically independent of, among other things, 'every morphological and behavioural, every phenotypic and genetic fact about Gustav'. Now, whatever 'primitive and irreducible' means, on the conception of properties as functions from individuals to sets of worlds (and remember that Schiffer intends his argument to apply quite generally to all conceptions of properties as language-independent entities) it cannot mean that ω is logically independent of all other properties. For suppose that

(65) $w \in \omega_1(a)$ iff a is a dog with large ears
(66) $w \in \omega_2(a)$ iff a is a dog without large ears.

Then even if ω (i.e. being a dog) is primitive and irreducible it is still the case that

(67) $w \in \omega(a)$ iff $w \in \omega_1(a)$ or $w \in \omega_2(a)$

so ω is logically equivalent to the disjunction of ω_1 and ω_2. The point is that on this conception of property primitiveness and irreducibility are not ontological matters but are relative to your favoured theory about the order of analysis.

So the most that the dog/shmog case could establish is that the pragmatic account, that is, the account which says that (53) and (64) really do have the same meaning, but that they differ pragmatically, is wrong. If it is wrong then we must find a semantic analysis of (53) which gives it a different truth value from (64). And that is the same problem as giving a semantic analysis of (54) which gives it a different truth value from (58). On pages 77–85 I mentioned two ways of providing a semantics for (55). One is to take *water* as a quantifier-like operator meaning 'it is true of that which plays the water role that'. Then you can distinguish between

(68) *possibly water is XYZ*

which is true, and

(69) *water* λx(*possibly x is XYZ*)

which is false. This is because

(70) *water is XYZ*

is true in w iff what plays the water role in w is XYZ. And

(71) *water is H_2O*

is true in w iff what plays the water role in w is H_2O. When someone says that it is metaphysically necessary that water is H_2O what they mean is that in the real world

(72) *water* λx *necessarily x is H_2O*

is true because what plays the water role here is H_2O in all worlds. Since (71) is a contingent proposition it can provide the content of Oscar's belief. The problem with this way of dealing with (55) is that it depended on a rather special syntactic characterization of words like *water*. While that characterization can be independently justified it does not generalize easily. We saw on page 80 that it didn't work for **whistles** and it is not clear that it would work for **dog** in analysing (53). The more general account made use of double indexing, and the rule for **water** was (36) on page 83. But whichever of these solutions is adopted, they both make use of the idea that there is such a thing as playing the water role. One might doubt that there is such a thing, and it certainly seems likely that one could not give a precise *definition* in more basic terms of just what it is to play the water role. However if (55) is to make any sense there must be such a thing, and that (55) does make sense is one of the facts that we are supposed to account for.

In $\mathscr{L}$ **dog** will be a one-place predicate and our task is to provide a double-indexed semantics for it. By analogy with V(**whistles**) stated in (45) on p. 84 it would have the semantics

(73) $\langle w, w' \rangle \in V(\textbf{dog})(a)$ iff a in w is in the kind which plays the dog role in w'.

Suppose that in the real world w_1, *Canis familiaris* plays the dog role. As this is a natural kind suppose that if a is a member of that kind in any world then it is a member of that kind in every world in which it exists. Also assume that Gustav is a dog in w_1. Take **is a dog** to have the same meaning as **dog** and take **necessarily** to be the dual of **possibly**, i.e. for $p \subseteq$ W,

(74) $w \in V(\textbf{necessarily})(p)$ iff for every w' such that $w R w'$, $w' \in p$.

Then consider the sentence

(75) **necessarily Gustav is a dog**

Assume that **Gustav** is a proper name whose meaning is simply Gustav. Then (75) will have the following semantics:

(76) $\langle w_1, w_1 \rangle \in V(75)$

iff, for every w such that $w_1 R w$,

(77) $\langle w, w_1 \rangle \in V(\textbf{Gustav is a dog})$

Then (77) holds iff

(78) $\langle w, w_1 \rangle \in V(\textbf{dog})(\text{Gustav})$

iff Gustav is a member of the natural kind that plays the dog role in w_1. Now the kind that plays this role in w_1 is *Canis familiaris* and because Gustav is a dog in w_1 then Gustav is a member of this kind, and since membership of a kind is essential to the members of the kind this means that Gustav is also a member of this kind in w. So (75) is true.

But suppose we say that it might have turned out that Gustav wasn't a dog - meaning by that that we might have discovered that all the things we thought to be dogs, including Gustav, were really robots. To get this sense we need the † operator mentioned on page 83, and we replace (75) by

(79) **necessarily †Gustav is a dog**

(79) will be true at $\langle w_1, w_1 \rangle$ iff, for every $w \in \text{W}$,

(80) $\langle w, w_1 \rangle \in \text{V}(\dagger)\text{V}(\textbf{\textit{Gustav is a dog}})$

iff

(81) $\langle w, w \rangle \in \text{V}(\textbf{\textit{dog}})(\text{Gustav})$

iff Gustav is a member of whatever it is that plays the dog role in w. Now we know that Gustav is a dog in every world. But in w_2, which we may suppose is possible relative to w_1, it will not be Gustav who plays the dog role since in w_2 what plays the dog role are not dogs but robots. So (81) is false when w is w_2, and so (79) is false at $\langle w_1, w_1 \rangle$.

To apply this to belief we make use of the idea of a doxastic alternativeness relation. Such a relation will be discussed in more detail on page 134 below. Using such a relation in the case of belief may well be an idealization but its combination with a double-indexed semantics does enable a solution to the problem of (53). For we take the semantics of **Tanya believes that** to be just like that of (74) except that $w\text{R}w'$ iff w' is one of Tanya's doxastic alternatives in w. Then (53) may be formalized as

(82) **Tanya believes that †Gustav is a dog**

The discussion of (79) can be paralleled for (82).

All this works, but it does depend on the idea of what it is to play the dog role. I have no analysis to offer of this. What I shall do instead is argue that an analysis is not required. If Putnam-type examples really do make sense in the first place then there really must be worlds in which it turns out that certain things are not dogs, and the property of playing the dog role is the property whose extension, in each world, is just the things that are not dogs but which dogs might have turned out to be. That such properties may have to be taken as primitive and undefinable is, as I have already remarked, no objection to their ontological status.

Schiffer does not consider the double-indexed solution to the problem posed by (53) but he does consider, on pages 65-9, a modification of the 'classical semantics'. I have already suggested that Schiffer has confused (61) and (62) but presumably he thinks that neither (61) nor (62) is true in all of Tanya's doxastic alternatives, since she may know no biology. What might be true is that there is some description *the P* (p. 65) which is satisfied by *Canis familiaris* and is such that Tanya believes that Gustav is a member of the kind that satisfies *the P*. Schiffer (p. 60) observes correctly that not every description will work. Suppose *the P* is 'the same species as the species of George's pet'. George's pet *is* a dog but Tanya thinks it is a goldfish. So Tanya does not believe that Gustav is a member of the kind that satisfies *the P*. The description therefore must in some sense be 'suitable'. Schiffer's complaint amounts to the claim there doesn't seem to be any account of when a description is suitable. Since he seems to be looking for a general account of suitability it is perhaps not surprising that there may be none to be had, though again he does not distinguish between the question of whether there is a class of suitable descriptions and the question of whether we can give a definition of that class. However, the double-indexing solution makes it a matter of the meaning of each particular natural-kind term just what kinds of things could count as playing the same role in other worlds as the things which satisfy the term in this world play in this world. If there *were* no such relation then there would be no problem in the first place. That we can give no account of it is neither here nor there.

The upshot of this chapter is that Putnam's work on the semantics of natural-kind terms, however interesting and important, poses no threat to possible-worlds semantics, and still leaves the issue of determining what counts as the intended interpretation of the language of a given population exactly where it was.

7

Lewis on languages and language

One of the few authors who has attempted to address the question of what it is about the linguistic behaviour of a population which justifies our saying that some particular model-theoretic interpretation is the right one for the language they speak is David Lewis (1975). Since I have already used $\mathcal{L}$ for a syntactically specified language I will use $\mathcal{L}^+$ for a language together with its interpretation rather than Lewis's $\mathcal{L}$. Lewis's proposal is (Lewis 1975, p. 7)

the convention whereby a population P uses a language $\mathcal{L}^+$ is a convention of *truthfulness* and *trust* in $\mathcal{L}^+$. To be truthful in $\mathcal{L}^+$ is to act in a certain way: to try never to utter any sentences of $\mathcal{L}^+$ that are not true in $\mathcal{L}^+$. Thus it is to avoid uttering any sentence of $\mathcal{L}^+$ unless one believes it to be true in $\mathcal{L}^+$. To be *trusting* in $\mathcal{L}^+$ is to form beliefs in a certain way: to impute truthfulness in $\mathcal{L}^+$ to others, and thus to tend to respond to another's utterance of any sentence of $\mathcal{L}^+$ by coming to believe that the uttered sentence is true in $\mathcal{L}^+$.

Where Lewis speaks of an interpreted language, which I have represented by $\mathcal{L}^+$ in quoting him, I prefer to speak of a language $\mathcal{L}$, together with an interpretation $\langle W,D,V \rangle$. I shall assume that speakers of $\mathcal{L}$ are members of D and that their properties and the relations among themselves and to other things are all appropriate set-theoretical entities constructed out of W and D. In particular, their beliefs may be construed as relations to propositions. Belief will therefore be a function ω such that for any $a \in D$, $p \subseteq W$ and any $w \in W$, $w \in \omega(a,p)$ iff a in w believes the proposition p. One might ask what it is to believe p, but the question would be premature. Lewis's strategy is in the tradition beginning with Grice 1957, which is to assume we know what believing is and use that to give an account of meaning. One could perhaps go further in assuming that every person a in every world w (at a time, if $\mathcal{L}$ were not so primitive as to avoid any temporal locutions) has a set of doxastic alternatives so that w' is a doxastic alternative of w iff nothing a believes in w rules out w'.

(See page 34 below and pages 28–36 of Lewis 1986a for a more elaborate account.)

We can now state Lewis's account in the terminology used earlier. $\langle W,D,V \rangle$ is the right interpretation for $\mathscr{L}$ as used by a population P in a world $w^\star$ provided there is a convention among the members a of P in $w^\star$ that:

(1) For any sentence α of $\mathscr{L}$, if a utters α in $w^\star$ then $w^\star \in \omega(a,V(\alpha))$
(2) $w^\star \in \omega(a,\{u{\in}W{:}\forall b{\in}P\ \forall\alpha(\alpha$ is a sentence of $\mathscr{L}$ and b utters α in $w \supset w \in \omega(b,V(\alpha)))\})$

Clause (2) is a bit baroque and further I suspect doesn't capture quite what Lewis says. All it means is that a believes that every member of P is attempting to be truthful. Clause (2) departs a little from Lewis. Lewis requires that the hearer trust the speaker to be speaking truly, i.e. he would require that in (2) a believe that if b utters α then $V(\alpha)$ is true in $w^\star$. This is because he thinks (see p. 8) that we commonly have reason to believe that the speaker's beliefs are correct. Either Lewis is right about this or he is wrong. If he is right then (2) gives us reason to trust that what the speaker says is true. If he is wrong then all a hearer should be willing to conclude is that the speaker believes the sentence to be true. This account depends not only on our having an analysis of belief, but also our having an analysis of a convention. Lewis 1975 uses an analysis of a convention adapted from Lewis 1969, and I shall later need to invoke this, but for the moment I don't propose to comment on it. It does make reference to beliefs, but that is not a worry because the aim of Lewis's paper is to give an account of meaning in terms of beliefs and other such attitudes. I have stated Lewis's theory in the terminology of $\mathscr{L}$ and $\langle W,D,V \rangle$ to shew how it applies to what I have said on pages 5-29 though many of my comments will not depend on the particular form that the theory takes. Lewis defends the theory against a number of objections. Mostly I think his replies are successful, and I shall concentrate on what I take to be the two major issues. The first issue concerns the necessity for truthfulness and trust, while the second concerns its sufficiency. The objections on the score of necessity (and Lewis lists them himself) concern the fact that on many occasions people use language for other purposes than to communicate what they believe, and their hearers know this and do not take them to be communicating beliefs. There are two kinds of case to consider. One is where there are syntactic indications of mood. Lewis defines what he calls a *polymodal* language on p. 14. An indicative sentence means what it does in accordance with (1) and (2). According to Lewis, to be truthful with respect to imperatives is to try to make them true when addressed by someone in authority over you. (This seems too strong to me. It would seem sufficient that you come to believe the speaker is trying to get you to do something. However I am not taking issue with the details.) To be trusting with respect to imperatives is to expect those in your authority to make them true. Presumably to be truthful with respect to interrogatives is to wish to know the answer to whether the sentence is true or false, or to what things satisfy a predicate.

The problem with this is with the notion of mood. What Lewis is saying is that when the syntax of $\mathscr{L}$ provides α with a mood indicator an utterance of α is to satisfy a condition of truthfulness and trust different from that associated with another mood marker. But there could well be languages in which mood is not syntactically marked. And even in English orders can be expressed by indicative sentences. On page 229 of Cresswell 1973 I instanced

(3)   The boy who is responsible will report to my office at nine o'clock tomorrow.

One might respond by saying that in a context in which (3) is being given as an order then, whether or not there is any syntactic marking of this, the utterance in question is to be assessed as if it were an imperative. I think this response is a good one, and I would like to generalize it. I am less sure that it is Lewis's response. The reason I would like to generalize this response is that I think it can be used to cover situations Lewis discusses on pages 27-9 where language is used deceitfully, ironically, metaphorically, in joking, in storytelling and so on. The idea would be something like this. If *a* utters a sentence α of $\mathscr{L}$ deceitfully then it means *p* provided *p* is not what *a* believes but what *a* wants the addressee to think *a* believes. If *a* utters *p* in a story then it means that *a* wants the audience to imaginatively entertain what the story says, and so on. The point of this theory is that, unlike Lewis's, it does not try to say once and for all what the purpose of language is, but supposes that we have independent evidence, in particular cases, of just what is supposed to be going on. Here's how it might go in a particular example of a directive use of $\mathscr{L}$.

In the directive use a sentence is uttered and an action follows. Perhaps the action is a linguistic action, as it could be in response to the directive

(4)   Tell me the capital of Peru.

But it need not be. Consider the following situation. A says

(5)   Wash a lettuce

and B washes a lettuce. How can this fact be used as evidence that (5) in English means that B is to wash a lettuce? The description so far won't do it on its own, since B could be rebellious and the lettuce washing be a way of defying A in whose language (5) means what

(6)   wash a potato

means in English. In order to conclude something about the meaning of (5) on the basis of B's response we need to know that B has heard A correctly, is willing to respond, is able to respond and responds because of what A's sentence means. In other words we must know that the situation is, in a sense, felicitous. The analysis of just what counts as felicitous is what is missing, and it may seem that the whole notion of meaning is presupposed, but this is not so because the analysis will not be sufficient to deliver on its own the meaning of (5). The assumption of felicity simply means that B's action in response to A's utterance can be regarded as establishing the meaning of (5). In what way is this so? It is the mark of a felicitous circumstance that A's utterance of (5) causes, in the circumstances, B's response. For we can say that had A not uttered (5) then B would not have washed a lettuce.

What we do is tell this story for all the possible uses of language that there are. Then we notice what they all have in common. It is that each use of language involves some appropriate relation to a proposition. It is this common element which justifies the truth-conditional core of semantics. I shall, in the next chapter, make the case for saying that the reason for this is that what justifies content ascription are the causal connections between speakers and things, but causal connections in the everyday sense of cause in which the terms of causal statements - typically expressed by 'because' - are propositions.

I am not sure whether this theory is Lewis's though it seems to me very much in the same spirit. On page 28 Lewis replies to the objection about irony, metaphor, hyperbole and so on in a way I do not entirely understand and seems to want to make the same reply in the case of story-telling. To the extent that I do understand it it seems to go something like this. If I say

(7)   One thing was certain, that the *white* kitten had had nothing to do with it

then, if I am beginning a story, I am presumably not saying this because I believe it, and you do not trust me to believe it. But, given that the context makes it clear that I am story-telling, then I am being truthful and trusting in another language. That is the language in which (7) means

(8)   It is true in the story being told in the context that one thing was ... etc.

and it is *this* that I believe (since I am the story-teller I make it true, and therefore believe it, by stipulation) and that you trust me to believe. This theory may not be quite the one I illustrated with the washing lettuce example, but it is similar to it in this respect. It is the utterance context which tells you what attitudes are appropriate to speaker and hearer. Either it does this directly or it does this by telling you to use a different language.

Now to the issue of the *sufficiency* of truthfulness and trust. One of the commonest complaints against a Gricean theory of meaning was that it gave no hint as to how compositionality is involved. Grice 1968 attempted to say something about this, but the result was hardly satisfactory. (For some interesting remarks on this see Grandy 1982.) Lewis discusses compositionality on pages 18-21 in his reply to an objection which begins at the bottom of page 17. Essentially his reply is that what he calls a grammar Γ will be the correct grammar if it generates meanings for the sentences which satisfy the convention of truthfulness and trust. By a 'grammar' Lewis includes an interpretation, and so, in our terms, Γ would consist of $\mathscr{L}$ with all its syntactical rules, together with some particular $\langle W,D,V \rangle$. This has in fact been built in to the version that I stated for $\mathscr{L}$ and $\langle W,D,V \rangle$ above.

However, if we look back at (1) and (2) we see that all that could possibly be fixed by these clauses is the truth conditions of whole sentences. For suppose that $\langle W,D_1,V_1 \rangle$ and $\langle W,D_2,V_2 \rangle$ have the property that for every *sentence* α of $\mathscr{L}$

(9) $V_1(\alpha) = V_2(\alpha)$

Then $\langle W,D,V_1 \rangle$ will satisfy (1) and (2) iff $\langle W,D,V_2 \rangle$ does, and so each will be correct iff the other is. Lewis is aware of this possibility and he considers replacing his strategy by a strategy which begins by defining what it is for a grammar Γ to be the grammar of a population, and then says that a sentence α of the language used by the population has a particular meaning iff it has that meaning according to Γ. Lewis rejects this way of proceeding because he sees no way to make objective sense of the assertion that some grammar Γ rather than a different grammar Γ' is the correct one where Γ and Γ' give exactly the same truth conditions to sentences. He is prepared to tolerate an indeterminacy here and claims that his purpose will be served provided he can use propositional attitudes to determine the meaning of full sentences.

In my view the situation is a little more serious because of the version of the isomorphism problem discussed on page 41 above in which $\langle W, D_1, V_1 \rangle$ and $\langle W, D_4, V_4 \rangle$ share the same worlds but in which their domains of individuals differ and so do their value assignments. One language might be talking about people running while another is talking about numbers satisfying a complex mathematical property. I suspect that when Lewis talks about Γ and Γ' he has in mind grammars which differ at a theoretical level, not the difference between a language in which **runs** refers to running and one in which **runs** refers to a property of numbers. One might be able to provide a partial solution to this problem by taking seriously the role of demonstration in utterances. If I point at David and say

(10) Look, he's running

I might be held to have done more than merely utter a sentence. I have uttered it in the context of demonstrating David. Since David is not a number this rules out $\langle W, D_4, V_4 \rangle$ in favour of $\langle W, D_1, V_1 \rangle$. Lewis discusses indexical languages on pages 13-16 and it might be that (10) will come under his account if we say that believing (10) to be true in a context is believing running of the indicated object in that context. (Perhaps the causal theory of reference might help here. I make a few remarks about this on page 129.) This solution would not deal completely with the isomorphism problem since there is no reason to suppose that everything in the universe can be demonstratively indicated or will have a name in $\mathscr{L}$. Whether the level of indeterminacy remaining ought to be worrying is a delicate matter on which I find the evidence unclear.

A different kind of objection arises from the fact that many sentences of $\mathscr{L}$ will never be uttered. Before I comment on this objection I shall mention a difficulty which still arises even if, *per impossibile*, every sentence of $\mathscr{L}$ *were* uttered by a member of P in w. Suppose that we have to adjudicate between $\langle W, D_1, V_1 \rangle$ and $\langle W, D_4, V_4 \rangle$, but suppose that α is a sentence which is uttered only once, by some $a \in P$, and that no one else believes that α is ever uttered, and that a believes that it is never uttered except on that one occasion. Suppose further that *a* believes in *w both* $V_1(\alpha)$ *and* $V_4(\alpha)$. Of course *a* will not recognize both propositions as meanings of α, but they are still among *a*'s beliefs. So P's beliefs will not determine which belief is the one expressed by α. For Lewis's definition to work in respect of α there must be a regularity between utterances of α and a particular belief sufficiently general for it to count as conventional. It will not do to get this extra generality by making the 'if' in (1) a counterfactual. For if *a* in *w* does not utter α we cannot reason from what beliefs *a* would have had if *a* did utter α, because we cannot be sure that in such a case *a* is speaking the same language. The word 'robin' in British English is supposed to mean something different from what it means in American English. Suppose David, an Englishman, has just been telling Julie that if he were brought up in America he would probably have been an ornithologist and would have been talking all the time about robins. Julie, speaking American English, says

(11) If David had uttered 'Robins are red' he would have believed that robins are red.

Julie knows that David is a speaker of British English whose upbringing ensures that the only way he would ever have talked about robins would be if he had been brought up in America and been speaking a different version of English from the version he does speak.

So even if all sentences *were* uttered it would still not be sufficient to determine a correct interpretation. In any case it is clear that many sentences of a natural language are never uttered. Hawthorne (1990) makes the following objection to Lewis. For every English sentence α that is too long for any speaker to utter it is trivially true that if uttered the speaker would believe that *p* for any proposition *p* whatever. Since Lewis insists that a regularity is a convention only if it rather than an alternative regularity obtain, it cannot be a convention that the population uses α only when they believe *p*.

This issue raises a question I briefly mentioned when discussing the syntax of categorial languages. In terms of syntactic category it is names and sentences which are simple and functors which are complex. Lewis's recipe, possibly augmented by demonstrative utterances, provides us with a way of getting at the meaning of names and sentences which at least constrains, if it does not determine, the meanings of functors. Imagine that we want to establish the meaning of a one-place predicate Φ. If we have established that *a* has a name N in $\mathscr{L}$ we can say $V(\Phi)(a) = V(\Phi N)$, and in general if δ is a functor in category $(\sigma/\tau_1...\tau_n)$ and we know that $a_1,...,a_n$ are the semantic values of expressions $\alpha_1,...,\alpha_n$ in categories σ, $\tau_1,...,\tau_n$ respectively, then we may say that $V(\delta)(a_1,...,a_n) = V(\delta\alpha_1...\alpha_n)$. Since complex syntactic categories are obtained from simpler ones by the process indicated this gives values for expressions of every category.

But this is only one dimension of simplicity and complexity. The other dimension is that symbols, which can be of any category, are simple, and complex expressions (which also can be of any category) are made up out of them. The tension between these two dimensions is relevant to the present issue. The reason we say that the unuttered sentences of English have the meanings they do is because the symbols in them have the meanings *they* do, and the meanings of the unuttered sentences are determined, according to Frege's Principle, by the meanings of their symbols and their grammatical structure. The tension arises because on Lewis's account the meaning of the separate symbols is constituted by the fact that they make a particular contribution to the meanings of whole sentences.

This tension may not be an inconsistency. One might say that the reason we are *able* to produce sentences of $\mathscr{L}$ in a way which satisfies (1) and (2) is because they are complex entities constructed out of simpler parts but that an account of *what it is* that we are able to do is to produce whole sentences in accordance with (1) and (2). Still the tension could cause difficulties in the following way. If Lewis is right, given the normal English meaning of

(12) *Adriane whistles*

English speakers only utter (12) if they believe that Adriane whistles, and trust other speakers to do the same. Consider then an English speaker who wants to convey the belief that Adriane whistles. There would seem to be two possibilities. Suppose (12) is one of the sentences which have been uttered sufficiently frequently for us to say that there is a convention that it be uttered only when the speaker believes that Adriane whistles and a convention to trust others to do the same. If that is what constitutes its meaning what it does, then it would seem that the utterer who wants to convey the belief that Adriane whistles by uttering (12) would have to know that this convention exists, and that seems to require that the utterer know that (12) has been uttered enough times to establish the existence of this convention.

This is clearly too strong. For recall that we are assuming that the speaker's *knowledge* of the meaning of (12) is obtained compositionally - this is what Lewis acknowledges even though he seems not to want to admit that *what it is that they know* is a compositional fact. But it is surely clear that knowledge of the meaning of **Adriane** and the meaning of **whistles** cannot lead you to the knowledge that (12) has been uttered often enough to establish a convention linking it with Adriane's whistling.

And of course the second possibility is that (12) has *not* been uttered sufficiently often for this purpose, and then what the speaker must know is presumably that the best grammar that accords with the convention of truthfulness and trust in $\mathscr{L}^+$ is one which associates with (12) the set of worlds in which Adriane whistles. But notice what this entails. It entails that the fact that what the utterer of (12), or any other user of the language, knows in knowing the meaning of (12) is that it has the truth conditions specified by the best grammar justified by the convention of truthfulness and trust.

The problem here is with the notion of best grammar. Lewis 1975, p. 20, claims that he knows of no promising way of making a choice between two grammars which generate the same language, and for that reason makes his convention of truthfulness and trust to be in a language and not a grammar. But the lesson that I suggest we learn from (12) is that what a speaker of a language can reasonably be expected to *know* is that the grammar which best generalizes a convention known to the speaker up to that point associates certain truth conditions with (12). Perhaps I can make the point clearer by looking at some variants of (12):

(13) **Bruce whistles**
(14) **Adriane runs**

Suppose that (12)–(14) have all been uttered sufficiently often to establish a convention of truthfulness and trust in them. Let us describe what this means in terms of Lewis's account. From now on I shall speak only in terms of the truthfulness part, since my points will be unaffected by the addition of the trust part. So the following regularity obtains among population P: they utter (12), (13) and (14) only when they believe, respectively, that Adriane whistles, that Bruce whistles, and that Adriane runs. Let us assume that the simplest grammar which gives these sentences the corresponding truth conditions also gives, as its semantic value,

(15) **Bruce runs**

the set of worlds in which Bruce runs. If what I said before is correct it is *this* that the utterer, S, of (15) knows who knows its meaning.

What I will claim is this. The point of the convention of truthfulness and trust in $\mathscr{L}$ is to predict not only that (15) has certain truth conditions determined by the best grammar that respects the convention governing (12)–(14), but also that (15) itself can be (and presumably will be, or would be) used only when S believes that Bruce runs. So the question is whether we can get from the convention governing (12)–(14) to the corresponding convention governing (15). In Lewis's terms this means that we are given that

(16) There is a regularity connecting the utterances of (12)–(14) and the relevant beliefs.

(17) Members of P believe that others conform to (16).

(18) This belief gives members of P a reason to conform themselves.

Lewis has a number of other conditions, such as that there be a preference for general conformity to (16) rather than slightly-less-than-general conformity, that (16)–(18) be mutual knowledge, that alternative regularities be possible, and so on. But it will be sufficient to look at (16)–(18) and see what happens when we try to extend them to (15).

For the convention to extend to (15) it is not sufficient merely that it be uttered only under the appropriate conditions. Condition (17) requires that members of P should know this. As in the case of (12) we can imagine two possibilities. It might be that (15) has been frequently uttered, and the question is whether what S knows about (12)–(14) gives good evidence to suppose that (15) has only been uttered when its speakers believe that Bruce runs. The answer, surely, is that it does *if* we may suppose that it is the best grammar which fits (12)–(14) which is causally efficacious in restricting the productions of (15) to cases in which S believes that Bruce runs. Thus (17) requires that members of P believe that the best grammar is causally efficacious. If they believe that then this belief certainly gives them a reason to conform, at least it does so if the corresponding beliefs about (12)–(14) give them a reason to conform. And what all *this* entails is that *if* the convention of truthfulness (and trust) in respect of (12)–(14) is to give reason for belief in a similar convention applied to (15) then the convention must be, on Lewis's analysis of convention, to speak according to a particular grammar, in fact according to that grammar which has been described as the best grammar that generates truth conditions which fit the convention as applied to those actually uttered sentences on which it is based.

Suppose then that we analyse (12) according to the syntax of $\mathscr{L}$ as set out in chapters 1 and 2. Is it possible to state a convention governing the use of individual words which will have the consequence that those sentences which are uttered frequently enough are uttered only in circumstances in which the utterer believes the proposition which has the truth conditions specified by the grammar? In tackling this I shall make a simplifying assumption. It is not an innocent assumption, as I noted on page 99, but it will get us started more easily. I shall assume that we already have an account of what it is for every name N in $\mathscr{L}$ to denote the individual it does denote in the language spoken by the members of P. The kind of convention we require must at least entail that every name N which is such that

(19) N *whistles*

has been uttered sufficiently often, is only uttered when *a* is the thing denoted by N, and that this fact is known to speakers of $\mathscr{L}$. But presumably more must be required, since, for reasons already given, the convention must give a reason to conclude this, whether or not you know that the sentence has been uttered. Provided we can make sense of the counterfactual supposition that members of P are still speaking the same language then we can presumably say that if (19) *were* to be uttered then its utterer would believe that *a* whistles. And the authority for this would be that members of P are speaking according to the grammar.

How might a grammar do this? An answer to this question is not strictly required if our concern, as it is, is simply with saying what counts as meaning whistling by *whistles* in the language spoken by P. But one should certainly be able to have some account of how it is that speakers should be able to do what we say they are doing when they speak their language. Whatever in detail is going on, and that is a matter for cognitive science, the grammar must be presumed to be giving the speaker some sort of conditional instruction like:

(20) Do not utter N *whistles* unless you believe that *a* whistles

and we may suppose, along the lines of Lewis's account of convention, that speakers regularly follow these instructions, that they believe that others do, and so on.

The procedure just described does of course depend on being able to establish that a name denotes what it does, and, as mentioned on page 99, one version of the isomorphism problem shews that no determination of truth conditions for whole sentences will force a name to denote what it does. I suggested there that an account of the activity of demonstrating an object might go some way towards solving this problem. I am not certain however that Lewis would solve the problem this way. In his reply to Hawthorne (Lewis 1992) he assumes that some grammars are just more reasonable than others. I guess that in the case of $\langle W_1, D_1, V_1 \rangle$ and $\langle W_4, D_4, V_4 \rangle$, on page 41 he would say that if you look at the circumstances in which a sentence like (7) or (8) on page 42 is uttered, while it may be true that in those circumstances the number of French hens is related in a certain way with the number of arrows which missed a certain target, yet anyone looking at the circumstances would be able to say that this is not a reasonable relation, and that the only reasonable relation involves circumstances in which Adriane runs or is seen by Bruce.

The use of (19) in establishing the meaning of **whistles** does raise problems regarding unnamed individuals. **whistles** may not be so bad here, at least if we assume that only people can whistle, since people typically do have names. But a predicate like

(21) *is within 100km of Mt Cook*

will certainly be true of many things which never have and never will be named. Notice that this is more difficult than the case of *sentences* involving (21). Such sentences will involve things that have been named. What we have to suppose is that linguistic usage is sufficiently precise that we can say of any unnamed thing what an utterer would have to believe who *did* use a name for it and uttered

(22) N *is within 100km of Mt Cook*

This way of establishing the meaning of predicates depends on taking names as in category n. There is however a phenomenon known as 'type raising', discussed on pages 131f. of Cresswell 1973, whereby a natural-language name can be thought of as the same category as a quantifier and put in category (s/(s/n)), and in general any expression of category τ can be mimicked by (or, alternatively, seen as) an expression in category $(\sigma/(\sigma/\tau))$ for any category σ. Thus, for instance, corresponding to the name **David**, whose semantic value is David (i.e., if V is the intended interpretation then V(**David**) is David), is the 'quantifier' **David**★ which means 'it is true of David that' in the same way that *everyone* means 'it is true of everyone that'. More precisely, for $\omega \in D_{(s/n)}$, and $w \in W$,

(23) $V(\textbf{David*})(\omega) = \omega(\text{David})$

Given this type raising one can achieve a plausible syntactic unification by treating all names as symbols in category $(s/(s/n))$; though in a language with variable-binding, say by λ-abstraction, one would need variables if not constants in category n.

This procedure affects (19) in the following way. It requires that we can select, from all the expressions in category $(s/(s/n))$, those which *could* be replaced by expressions in category n, and are able to identify which member of D each expression denotes. This is a consequence of the fact that the subject term simply denotes an individual. This fact is I suppose a little ironical in that the original motivation for putting the *meaning* of a one-place predicate in $D_{(s/n)}$ was that the predicate itself is in category (s/n) because it makes a sentence out of a name. The language $\mathscr{L}$ of course does have names in category n.

Suppose then that there is a convention of truthfulness and trust which says that for every $a \in D$, if N names a then utterers of (19) must believe that a whistles. What about symbols of higher category which take expressions in category (s/n) as values? One class of such expressions is quantifiers, expressions in category $(s/(s/n))$ whose semantics does not enable them to be replaced by any expression in category n. Another class is the class of predicate modifiers. These are in category $((s/n)/(s/n))$ and include both simple adverbs and complex adverbial phrases. Look first at quantifiers. For $\omega \in D_{(s/n)}$ and $w \in W$ we know that

(24) $w \in V(\textbf{everyone})(\omega)$ iff, for every person a, $w \in \omega(a)$.

Clearly (24) entails that $V(\textbf{everyone})$ only needs to know which individuals ω is true of to know how to operate on it, and putting predicates in category s/n and their meanings in $D_{(s/n)}$ makes that claim about all higher-order operators on predicates. Apparent counterexamples might come from propositional attitude contexts but I have argued in Cresswell 1985a that they should be treated differently.

How could (24) be established after the fashion of Lewis? You would have to say something like this. We assume that sentences like (19) can be used to establish the semantic values of all predicates. Suppose that Φ is such a predicate. Then *everyone* will mean everyone if there is a convention in P that you only utter

(25) *everyone* Φ

if you believe that everyone satisfies the property expressed by Φ.

In the case of (19) we had to account for unnamed individuals, because when a quantifier applies to a predicate it claims that the predicate is true of everything in the domain, not just those things which have names. In the case of (25) it is perhaps less clear that you need unnamed *predicates*. You would need them if there were higher-order sentences which genuinely quantified over predicates. Often, when that does appear to happen, as in sentences like

(26) Napoleon had all the qualities of a great general

the predicate is nominalized and its semantic value is a thing. Though even here it is a thing of the same kind as the semantic value of a predicate, and so our access to it should pose the same problems. (Of course (26) also poses self-reference problems, but I don't wish to say anything about those here.)

I have no argument of principle that this method of attributing word meanings won't work. The general procedure seems clear. If we have a way of establishing meanings for expressions in categories $\sigma, \tau_1, \ldots \tau_n$, then we obtain meanings in category $(\sigma/\tau_1 \ldots \tau_n)$ by looking at what the convention would be for the expression in category σ, obtained by prefixing (or infixing or suffixing) the operator whose meaning in P is to be established, to all possible arguments in $\tau_1, \ldots, \tau_n$. There are however a number of reservations about the procedure. This revision of Lewis means that we must use the convention of truthfulness and trust to establish the meaning of each word piecemeal. On Lewis's original view the grammar could be justified holistically as the best overall grammar which accords with the convention governing actually uttered sentences. Such holism is plausible in that I believe that one wants to be able to say that the meaning of an expression could be determined in all sorts of ways by the meanings of other expressions, some of which may well be of higher type. Perhaps a further revision will permit holism, though it is hard to see how if the convention must determine in each case the meaning of each word.

The most worrying thing about the revision is the amount of indeterminacy that it generates. Lewis felt that indeterminacy at the level of *grammars* might be unworrying since the issue was simply which grammar best generated the sentences conventionally uttered. But if, as I have argued, the grammar itself must be part of the convention then the gap between the detailed knowledge we surely have of the semantic structure of natural languages and the facts that the revision of Lewis's theory would deliver must raise the question of whether semantics can rest on such a shaky foundation. But if an account like Lewis's cannot deliver the results, what account can?

Well, perhaps an account which tries to argue that we can establish the meanings of individual words directly, and in the remainder of this chapter I want to consider the view that Tarski's theory of truth (Tarski 1936) effects a successful reduction of the semantic to the non-semantic without the need for going through propositional attitudes and the behaviour of linguistic communities. For this purpose I shall discuss Field 1972 and, on pages 128–30, Field 1978. Field argues that the reason Tarski thought that his work was important was that he thought it really did amount to a reduction of semantic notions to physicalistically acceptable notions, and, presumably, without going through any messy facts of a psychological or sociological nature of the kind we have been looking at in the explanation of meaning via attitudes, and attitudes via behaviour. Field argues that although Tarski was not successful in this yet he did succeed in reducing some semantic notions to others. Some of my comments about Field's paper will echo points made in Soames 1984, though I shall often be illustrating them using the language $\mathscr{L}$ and its interpretations discussed earlier. Some of the points are also made in chapter 2 of Stalnaker 1984.

In terms of $\mathscr{L}$ you can think of what Tarski did as providing a semantics for the part of it which is not concerned with possible worlds, and where the semantics for **and**, **not** and **if** is as described in (21)–(23) on page 24. There is also a clause for the quantifiers which makes use of the semantics of variable-binding. Field suggests two ways of looking at Tarski. The first is what he thinks Tarski ought to have said and he calls this Tarski★. In order to approach Tarski★ I shall contrast it with what has emerged in our discussion of Lewis 1975. The principal claim of that work was that the behaviour of language users determined the semantics of whole sentences and that the semantics of individual symbols was determined by the contribution they made to whole sentences. But, as noted, this involved a tension with the fact that sentences are complex entities whose meaning is determined by the meanings of the words in them. One way of reconciling this tension would be to give an account of what it is for the words (symbols) of the language of a population to mean what they do, and let the meanings of whole sentences be determined by that. This is what Field's Tarski★ does for the language of first-order predicate logic.

If you look at that part of $\mathscr{L}$ which makes no reference to possible worlds you will see that to specify the meaning of a name all we have to do is establish what it is the name of, and to specify the meaning of a predicate all we have to do is to specify the things that it is true of. (Field also has function symbols. These don't add any new problems, and in any case can be eliminated. Also there are the complexities involved in quantification.) Field uses the word 'denotes' to indicate the relation between a name and what it denotes and on page 349 he says that the denotation of a name 'c_k' is 'some fixed object that users of the language refer to when they use the name "c_k"'. For predicates there are similar facts which determine what the predicate applies to.

If we know all this then, says Field, if we apply the rules for the logical symbols (which for $\mathscr{L}$ means (21)–(23) on p. 24) we get the truth or falsity of all sentences. (In languages with individual variables a distinction is made between open formulae, which contain unbound, or free, variables and closed formulae, which do not. It is usually only closed formulae which are called sentences.) This method does, however, assume that the meanings of the logical constants are fixed in all interpretations. One reason why this may seem less important is that in logical languages they are usually not represented as English words (or words of any other natural language.) Thus for **not** Field uses $\sim$ and for **and** Field uses $\wedge$. We can then restate (22) on p. 24 as

(27) $(\alpha \wedge \beta)$ is true iff α is true and β is true.

But if we accept a point made by Soames 1984, p. 420 we can ask what justifies (27) rather than (28)?

(28) $(\alpha \wedge \beta)$ is true iff either α is true or β is true.

One tempting answer is simply to say that $\wedge$ is a logical constant whose meaning is stipulated by (27). The constant whose meaning is stipulated by (28) is written as $\vee$, and that's all there is to it. This response merely pushes the problem back. For given that the speakers of $\mathscr{L}$ use the word **and** we have to determine how they do it. If they use it in accordance with (27) we translate it as $\wedge$. If they use it in accordance with (28) we translate it as $\vee$. The problem of what **and** means, as used by speakers of $\mathscr{L}$, still remains.

In the semantics of $\mathscr{L}$ proposed earlier a clear distinction was made between principles like (30), (35) and (38), which determine the meanings of **not**, **and** and **if** and 'structural' principles like (38) which say how complex expressions are to be evaluated on the basis of the meanings of their parts. Of course even the structural rules could have been different. In the semantics for $\mathscr{L}$ presented earlier these rules were fixed for all interpretations, but of course instead of (39) on page 27 we might have had, say,

(29) $w \in V(\delta\alpha_1..\alpha_n)$ iff $w \notin V(\delta)(V(\alpha_1),.., V(\alpha_n))$.

(29) is a silly rule perhaps, but if speakers of $\mathscr{L}$ really did interpret their sentences this way it would have to be used. What we *can* say is that if the meanings of *all* the symbols are given, and if the interpretation of the structural rules is fixed, then the meanings of all sentences are fixed.

Does this fact affect Field's claims? Well, if you look at the languages Tarski studied you will see that it originally seemed that all you had to do was establish

(30) Which things are named by the speakers of $\mathscr{L}$
(31) Which things the predicates used by the speakers of $\mathscr{L}$ apply to.

Later in the article, pages 366f, Field seems to think that a causal theory of names, of the kind presented in Kripke 1972a, ought to help with (30). He says less about (31), and indeed (31) presents something of a problem for purely extensional languages, i.e. for languages whose semantics makes no reference to possible worlds.

The problem can be seen by contrasting the situation in an extensional interpretation with what happens in an intensional interpretation when possible worlds are involved. Then we can see that the connection between **runs** and the set of those whom the predicate applies to is determined by two factors. The linguistic behaviour of a population can determine what they mean by **runs**, but it cannot determine who runs. That is to say, for a given $\mathscr{L}$ and a single given $\langle W,D,V \rangle$, there could be two worlds w_1 and w_2 such that some individual a runs in w_1 but does not run in w_2. In determining what the extension of **runs** is in w_1 we have to answer two questions:

(32) Which is the correct $\langle W,D,V \rangle$ for the speakers of $\mathscr{L}$ in w_1?
(33) Given that $\langle W,D,V \rangle$ is the correct interpretation, which set $A \subseteq D$ is such that $a \in A$ iff $w_1 \in V(\textbf{\textit{runs}})(a)$?

110

Assuming that the V(***runs***) in the correct interpretation is the property of running then (33) is simply the question of who runs in w_1. And *that* question is presumably a straightforward physical question not involving any dubious psychological or sociological notions of the kind that (32) does. I have of course stated (32) in such a way as to make the meaning of ***runs*** dependent on establishing the right $\langle W,D,V \rangle$. When Field's approach is applied to an intensional language you would presumably be assuming that V(***runs***) could be established on its own. Be that as it may, I suspect that those working in an extensional language may be forgetting the difference between (32) and (33) and may be using the fact that (33) involves only physical notions to suppose that (31) does as well.

One thing Field does seem right about: all that Tarski★ did was reduce the semantics of complex expressions to the semantics of their simple symbols. So why did Tarski suppose he had done more? To see this look again at what Tarski★ did. Applied to the name ***Adriane*** in $\mathscr{L}$ Tarski★ would say:

(34) ***Adriane*** denotes some fixed object that users of $\mathscr{L}$ refer to when they use the name ***Adriane***.

Tarski, according to Field, proceeds by translating the symbols of $\mathscr{L}$ into English and then, supposing that speakers of $\mathscr{L}$ use ***Adriane*** to refer to Adriane, he can express (34) by

(35) ***Adriane*** denotes Adriane.

Now I discussed a version of (35) as (40) on page 17 in which I considered

(36) V(***Adriane***) = Adriane

What I said there was that you might think that (36) is right while

(37) V(***Adriane***) = Bruce

is wrong because in the metalanguage in which (35) and (36) are expressed the name ***Adriane*** and the person Adriane are referred to in the same way. In the model-theoretic account used earlier a clear distinction is made between the interpretation itself, which includes the entities that occur in it as semantic values, and a metalinguistic statement about the interpretation. By talking about a translation of the object language into the metalanguage the impression is very easily given that (36) is somehow 'obvious' and contentless, and therefore might seem to be providing a (spurious) argument in favour of (36), = (40) on page 17, over (44) on page 17. As was remarked in discussing these sentences there is nothing about the nature of the interpretations themselves to tell us that one is wrong and the other is right. Field's way of putting things seems to me to turn a fairly straightforward situation into an obscure one.

If (36), which is what (35) becomes in a semantics for $\mathscr{L}$, is used as a way of stating semantic facts, then it reduces semantic facts to logical facts. For suppose, as before, that the names of $\mathscr{L}$ are precisely *Adriane*, *Bruce*, *Julie* and *David*, and that they denote, in the intended interpretation $\langle W,D,V \rangle$, Adriane, Bruce, Julie and David. Then the question of why they denote what they do is just the question of why

(38) V = {⟨*Adriane*, Adriane⟩, ⟨*Bruce*, Bruce⟩, ⟨*Julie*, Julie⟩, ⟨*David*, David⟩}

is the function it is. (In (38) of course we have not specified the whole of V but only that part of V which takes names as arguments.) And I have already observed (p. 18) that that is a non-question.

When we come to predicates we have to remember that Tarski is working with an extensional language in which there is only the actual world. For that reason we make no reference to possible worlds at all, and the meaning of a one-place predicate is just the set of things the predicate applies to, of a two-place predicate the set of ordered pairs the predicate applies to, and so on. So, if only Bruce and Julie run in the actual world you would have

(39) V(*runs*) = {Bruce, Julie}

and if you ask why *runs* has *that* meaning in $\langle W,D,V \rangle$ then the answer will be simply that that is part of what it is for V to be the function that it is. The rules of combination applied to (38) and (39) will then determine such semantic facts as that

(40) *Adriane runs*

is false but

(41) *Bruce runs*

is true. Since these are mathematical facts we have achieved a reduction of semantic facts to non-semantic facts. (A point worth observing here is that the falsity of (40) and the truth of (41) in an extensional language are *mathematical facts* not physical facts. So Tarski's reduction, if successful, would reduce semantics to mathematics. Intensional interpretations do not have that consequence, in that, although it is a mathematical fact that a sentence in a given interpretation means what it does, the meaning is something which can be true in one world but false in another.)

There is a terminological question raised in note 24 on page 425 of Soames 1984. In making points very like the ones I have just been making, Soames claims that this way of doing things isn't quite like model-theoretic approaches, because it defines truth *simpliciter* rather than truth in a model. The reason that this is a terminological matter is just this. If you specify $\mathcal{L}$ purely syntactically then the same language can have more than one interpretation and the truth value of a sentence in one interpretation may be different from its truth value in another. Alternatively you can think of $\mathcal{L}$ as an *interpreted* language by thinking of it as a syntactically specified language together with an interpretation. In an interpreted language we may indeed speak of truth *simpliciter*. We must of course distinguish between truth in a model and truth in a world. An extensional interpretation supplies sentences with truth values. An intensional interpretation supples them with truth conditions in the form of sets of worlds, and the very same sentence in the very same interpretation can be true in one world and false in another.

Field's objection to Tarski's method is a little different. Field illustrates it with the concept of valency. The valency (or valence) of a chemical element is a numerical measure of its ability to combine with other elements. Thus it can be represented by a two-place predicate whose first argument is a chemical element and whose second is a number. If so then the meaning of **valency** can be represented as the set of pairs

(42) $\{\langle \text{potassium}, +1\rangle, \langle \text{sulphur}, -2\rangle, ..., \text{etc.}\}$

Field expresses this as a disjunctive condition for the truth of the sentence

(43) E has valency n

where E stands for an element and n a number. That makes it look as though the finiteness of the set is an issue. Example (42) makes it clear that it isn't. Field's claim is that while (42) might tell you what the valency of each element *is*, it won't tell you what valency means. For that you need a lot of chemical theory.

We can make the same point in the case of **runs**. While (39) might tell you who satisfies **runs** it will not tell you what **runs** means. Now this indeed is an objection to (39) but it doesn't seem to me relevant to the issue that divides Tarski and Tarski★. The problem about (39) is simply that knowing the extension of **runs** is neither necessary nor sufficient for knowing its meaning. What you must know is its intension. It may still be arguable that the intension captures all there is to meaning, but at least it doesn't suffer from the obvious objections to (39). Similarly with (42) as an account of (43). If we replace (42) by a function which associates the appropriate set of pairs with each world it is no longer so obvious that we don't capture the meaning of **valency**.

So what is the real problem with Tarski's method? It is simply the problem that we have been dealing with all the time. Tarski's method sets out a particular interpretation. Within that interpretation, or within that interpreted language if you make the interpretation part of the definition of the particular language, the semantic facts are as they are because the interpretation is what it is. But that fact goes no way to answering what it is that makes a particular interpretation the intended one. Soames I think (1984, p. 426) is inclined to say that that is not a semantic question. Say so if you like, but then you will find difficulty in supposing that someone who asks

(44) How do you say that snow is white in German?

is asking a semantic question. For surely (44) is asking what German sentence α is such that where $\langle W,D,V \rangle$ is the intended model for German speakers, $V(\alpha)$ is the set of worlds in which snow is white. (At least it is asking this in the framework of an intensional language $\mathscr{L}$.) This is not the mathematical fact that $V(\alpha)$ is what it is, it is the contingent fact that $\langle W,D,V \rangle$ rather than some other interpretation is the one intended by German speakers. So whatever Tarski's definition of truth has done it does not excuse us from addressing the questions that have exercised us in this and earlier chapters.

8

Causation and semantics

The principal claim of this chapter is that the account of causation appropriate to semantics is the one based on possible worlds. I shall in fact make use of the counterfactual analysis of causation developed by David Lewis. This account is stated in terms of possible worlds, and one of the things I shall be trying to shew is that the explanation for the success of possible-worlds semantics is that the causal facts which justify it are themselves to be expressed by means of possible worlds. Indeed what I shall be trying to shew is that it is the use of worlds in the analysis of counterfactuals that provides the strongest justification for their adoption in semantics.

In Lewis 1973b, the statement

(1) e_1 causes e_2

where e_1 and e_2 are events, is analysed in terms of a chain of *counterfactual dependencies* and is based on the counterfactual statement that if e_1 had not occurred then neither would e_2. If Oe_1 is the statement that e_1 occurs and Oe_2 that e_2 occurs then the counterfactual dependence is expressed by

(2) $\sim Oe_1 \; \Box\!\!\!\rightarrow \; \sim Oe_2$

where $\Box\!\!\!\rightarrow$ is Lewis's symbol for the counterfactual operator, and for schematic α and β,

(3) $\alpha \; \Box\!\!\!\rightarrow \; \beta$

is true in world w iff β is true in the closest world to w in which α is true. (Refinements are required to take care of cases in which there is no nearest world, and the degenerate case in which α is true at no world. See Lewis 1973a.) Where does nearness come from? Lewis often speaks of it as 'comparative overall similarity' but in Lewis 1979b, he recognizes that the way to investigate its nature is not to begin with ideas about similarity and then attempt to determine the truth conditions of counterfactual sentences – if we do that we shall frequently get those truth conditions wrong – but rather to use the truth conditions of counterfactual sentences to indicate what kind of a similarity relation is being used.

If a possible-worlds metaphysics is to be viable in using causation to naturalize semantics then the role of possible worlds in a naturalistic account of reality must be addressed. In chapter 5 I spoke about the metaphysics of possible worlds and in this chapter I shall only be concerned with the following question. It might be held that it is implausible, or at least contrary to the naturalistic spirit, to suppose that there is such a thing as an independent modal reality. In other words, there are no brute modal facts. All modal facts supervene on non-modal facts. Whether or not this is indeed so, it is something which many possible-worlds theorists are prepared to accept. Thus Lewis expresses sympathy with the view that a possible world is constituted by 'local matters of particular fact' (Lewis 1986b, p. ix), and I have myself used a *Tractatus*-like picture of possible worlds to articulate this (Cresswell 1973 ch. 3, and 1990, ch. 12; the next few pages draw on material from pp. 160-4 of Cresswell 1990). In its simplest version you have to imagine that the holding or not of each particular atomic situation is logically independent of the holding or not of any other atomic situation. For instance if it were plausible to think that everything about a possible world is determined by whether or not a particular point of space is occupied at a particular time, then a possible world could be a collection of spatio-temporal co-ordinates (or something more complex in a relativistic framework) and a 'sentence' in a basic physical language $\mathscr{L}$ containing only the predicate **occupied** and names for points of space and moments of time describing such a world would be a conjunction of atomic sentences of the form

(a) **Occupied** (p,t)

or

(b) $\sim$ **Occupied** (p,t)

where p is the name of a point of space and t of a moment of time (one of form (a) or (b), but not both, for each p and t). If a proposition is a set of worlds and a world can be represented by an infinite conjunction of (a)- or (b)-type sentences then any proposition can be represented by an infinite disjunction of infinite conjunctions. Such a sentence would not contain any modal primitives. So if α is a sentence in any language, even one containing modal words, it would in *theory* have a 'translation' into the basic physical language $\mathscr{L}$. But this is no ordinary notion of 'translation'. For the target sentences are infinite disjunctions of infinite conjunctions, and there is no reason to suppose that even if they were not there would be any effective way of obtaining the sentence of $\mathscr{L}$. So although the truth of any sentence in a language whose semantics involves possible worlds which can be described atomistically in $\mathscr{L}$ depends only on local matters of particular non-modal fact, yet there is no genuine sense in which sentences like (2) can be reduced to non-modal sentences.

One could put this by saying that although the modal *supervenes* on matters of particular fact, yet it is not *reducible* to such matters. This distinction is not primarily an ontological one, and indeed from an ontological point of view the present model may indeed be said to be one in which worlds are reduced to other things. But whatever problems there may be in formulating a supervenience/reduction distinction in general it seems relatively straightforward here. Supervenience amounts to a kind of logical dependence whereby two distinct worlds cannot coincide on all matters of particular fact; and yet it does not amount to reducibility, since there may be no sentence involving only predicates describing matters of particular fact which is equivalent to a given modal sentence.

In fact we don't need to go even as far as modality to see supervenience without reduction at work. Take a case in which even Quine (1960, p. 32) seems sympathetic to a notion of meaning – stimulus meaning. The single-word sentence 'gavagai' is uttered just when the language user receives a particular stimulation. My point is a little different from Quine's of course since he was concerned to shew that stimulus meaning is unable to distinguish between a rabbit as a repeatable entity or as a 'rabbit stage' which it makes no sense to identify with any other rabbit stage. But even in this attenuated case we can see how to have supervenience without reduction. We need not assume that the sentence is vague – there is a precise collection of matters of particular fact (maybe when enough space is occupied in the language user's vicinity) which always triggers the sentence off and which we may call its (stimulus) meaning. It is rather because the precise conditions which in fact cause a particular response in a particular extremely complex organism need not be ones which the organism is able to express in predicates which are part of the underlying physical theory in which it describes the world. They are just too complex.

The same is true in the modal case. In order to see how this can be I shall go through the analysis of (3) that you would get on the basis of David Lewis's 1973a semantics for counterfactuals. (For the purposes of this chapter differences between that account and others like that of Stalnaker are irrelevant.) In this version there is a three-place relation of what Lewis calls comparative 'overall similarity' and which is usually thought of metaphorically as closeness or nearness. Using this we specify the semantics for the counterfactual operator $\Box\!\!\rightarrow$ as:

$\alpha \; \Box\!\!\rightarrow \; \beta$ is true at a world w_1 iff there is a world w_2 at which α and β are both true, which is closer to w_1 than any world w_3 at which α is true but β is false.

We assume that α and β are true at certain times in certain worlds. The aim is to shew that, given that α and β depend only on the particular facts that make up the worlds in which they are true, then (3) will be true in a world w_1 solely on the basis of particular facts in w_1. What would it be for the truth of (3) at w_1 to depend on *more* than the matters of particular fact which hold? Well there would have to be a w_1 and a $w_1\star$ which coincide on all matters of particular fact, but where (say) w_2 is closer to w_1 than w_3 is, but w_2 is not closer to $w_1\star$ than w_3 is. But if w_1 and $w_1\star$ coincide on matters of particular fact they are identical, and so what is claimed cannot happen.

The reason we need to postulate a nearness relation for the analysis of counterfactuals is simply that no effective translation of a counterfactual into the basic physical language is possible. And even if we should allow ourselves all kinds of predicates, constrained only by their being predicates which in some sense report what is 'actually' the case, the prehistory of the analysis of counterfactuals (pre-Stalnaker 1968, that is) shews that no reductive analysis is plausible. By not insisting that the nearness relation among worlds be *defined* in terms of the particular facts of the worlds in question, counterfactuals can be accommodated without a reductive analysis, even when worlds are no more than collections of matters of basic particular fact. This does not mean that nearness does not depend on basic particular facts. Indeed, how could it fail to since, that is, all worlds are and nearness is a three-place relation among worlds? Nor does it mean that one cannot look for principles which constrain this relation, as David Lewis has done in Lewis 1979b.

The point about the unreducibility of nearness may apply to unreducibility in general, and may in fact underlie much of the need for abstract entities in semantics. For if we *could* give a reductive account of nearness, if we could say in terms of the physical predicates just *when* one world was nearer to a second than to a third, then we would not need the nearness relation, and presumably would not need the operation of forming arbitrary sets of basic particular facts. Abstract entities are the mechanism by which it is possible to have supervenience without reduction. And the complexity of features to which language users are sensitive provides a central reason why it is necessary to have supervenience without reduction.

There is though still a difference between the 'gavagai' case and the modal case. For even though the gavagai sentence may not be reducible to a sentence of $\mathscr{L}$ in any genuine sense yet it is experientially identifiable. In the modal case simply postulating a nearness relation does not give us any such access. Lewis has called this 'comparative overall similarity' but has wisely left it to our use of counterfactuals to determine what it is. I would like to focus on a use of counterfactuals which will prove important in what follows, namely their reliability as guides for action. This use is important because semantics is often held to have a close connection with propositional attitudes like belief and desire, and these in turn are supposed to get their meaning by providing causal explanations of behaviour. What I intend to shew is that the sense of cause involved in these explanations is the one that Lewis analyses, whether or not there are other senses of cause which may be more appropriate to fully developed scientific theories.

Now, the normal way of rendering $\alpha \ \Box\!\!\rightarrow \beta$ in English is by saying

(4) If it had been the case that α then it would have been the case that β.

and one way of understanding (4) is to go back to a time when it was still open for α to occur, even though in the real world α did not subsequently occur, and ask whether at that time it would have been true to say

(5) If α occurs then β will.

The connection between sentences like (4) and sentences like (5) has been studied in Dudman 1984. If we take seriously the *Tractatus*-like picture I have just presented then possible worlds are better seen as possible histories, and it is easy to think of two worlds which coincide on all their atomic facts up to a certain moment of time t, and diverge

119

thereafter. Suppose then that w is a world made up out of atomic facts in this way. A typical use of a sentence like (5) will involve an α which happens at a particular time, so that there will be a time t, such that if α is true in w it will also be true in every w_1 which coincides with w up to t. The simplest semantics for (5) would be just to say that it is true in w iff β is true in every w_1 which coincides with w up to just before t, but of course that would strengthen $\square\!\!\!\rightarrow$ to strict implication. The job of 'nearness' is to put constraints on the w_1's.

The point of looking at (5) rather than (4) is that it focuses on the role of counterfactuals in everyday life. I may be wondering whether or not to bring about β, and can reason that doing α is likely to achieve this. Or I can predict the behaviour of others using similar principles. This means that the nearness relation, if it is to be successful, must be reliable. Now if counterfactuals are to be used reliably we must be able to have evidence for their truth. And what evidence could we have for the truth of a sentence like (5)? Surely that in the past cases relatively similar to α are followed by cases relatively similar to β. Well not only that of course - the kind of evidence relevant to the truth of (5) can come from a wide variety of sources. For that reason there is no hope of letting the *meaning* of (5) be simply a statement about what has happened in the past. It is I believe this semantic requirement that forces us to think in terms of possible worlds. For the link between the truth of (5) and past experience must be made by postulating a connection between the way the world has been in the past and the way it will continue to be. The way I see the matter is this. We live I suppose in a world that in the past has been inductively reliable. What this means is that we have been able to describe it in terms which have enabled us to predict more or less reliably how the future would go on the basis of how the past went. The world may of course suddenly cease to be reliable - perhaps we live in a rogue world which will begin misbehaving tomorrow. One thing we know is that no evidence available to us can rule out the possibility that we are in a rogue world. Further there are as many if not more rogue worlds as reliable worlds. All we can do is assume that we are not in a rogue world. It seems to me a strength of possible-worlds metaphysics that it makes clear that the problem of induction is a real problem to which, as far as I am aware, there is no answer.

So I shall assume that in the evaluation of counterfactuals we restrict ourselves to those worlds which are such that there can be established a collection of properties which are inductively reliable in the sense that for any time t, the regularities which have obtained up to t continue to obtain after t. I am not able to be more precise than that. But it doesn't worry me because that seems to be everyone's problem. Now go back to the analysis of (5) and assume that its truth is to be evaluated in an inductively reliable world w_1. The definition of an inductively reliable world was that it was one in which cases relevantly similar to α are followed by cases relevantly similar to β. Two points emerge. First, similarity has entered the picture. So we can say that part at least of the similarity measure among worlds is how much of the regularities in the base world are preserved. The other point is that whether or not β can be reliably expected to follow α depends not just on α, but rather what, adapting a phrase of Lennart Åqvist's (1973) might be called α-in-the-circumstances. So the idea is that the closest α world to w is one in which things continue as they have done in most cases relevantly similar to α-in-the-circumstances. The special case in which w is an α world, and therefore is the closest world to itself requires that w be inductively reliable since only in that case can conditionals with true antecedents be reliable over time.

In looking at causal explanations based on counterfactuals we are in fact looking at cases in which α and β are both true, and the dependence of β on α in w is indicated by the truth in w of the counterfactual

(6) $\ \sim\alpha \ \square\!\!\rightarrow \ \sim\beta$

As an example take

(7) The water flowed because I turned on the tap.

The practical point of (7) is to help answer someone who says

(8) What must I do to make the water flow?

And the way it answers is to ensure that, in inductively reliable worlds, failing to turn on the tap in circumstances relevantly similar to the actual world will over time be correlated with failure of water flow. So relying on the truth of (7) will yield practical success in the long run. This is ensured by requiring that a world which is less well correlated with the inductive regularities of the base world is further from it than one which is more highly correlated. It is important to see that nearness is not being *defined* in terms of inductive reliability. At best it is constrained by it. I doubt whether any definition is possible, since if it were one could presumably define the truth conditions for $\square\!\!\rightarrow$ directly. The other point is that not all counterfactuals are like (5) and the point of the nearness relation is to provide a semantics which will work in all cases.

An explanation of behaviour in terms of beliefs and closeness will take some such form as this:

(9) Harry took the bus because he thought it was going to Northampton.

Counterfactually this can be expressed as

(10) If Harry had not thought it was going to Northampton he would not have taken the bus.

This is true iff Harry does not take the bus in the nearest world in which he fails to think it is going to Northampton.

Example (10) of course will not quite do as an account of (9) for well-known reasons. Suppose (I owe this example to Lynne Baker) that a bus to Sunderland would have done equally well, but it just happened that the Northampton bus came along first. Harry caught the bus because it was going to Northampton, but even if it hadn't been he would still have caught it, if it had been going to Sunderland. So (9) would be true but (10) false.

Solutions to this kind of problem all have the form of making the requirements for causation weaker than for counterfactual dependence. Lewis allows a chain of counterfactual dependencies to be a causal chain even if the last term does not counterfactually depend on the first. In the present example what seems to be going on is that (10) reports something which, given that the bus *was* going to Northampton, is not only sufficient in the circumstances for Harry's catching it, but also necessary in the circumstances, and it seems that a cause need only be something which is sufficient in the circumstances. It would be nice to be able to deal with this problem by saying that if α logically entails γ and α and β are both true in w and $\sim\gamma \ \Box\!\!\rightarrow \ \sim\beta$ is true in w then β because α is also true in w.

I have used 'because' rather than 'cause' here since part of my claim will be that the sense of 'cause' relevant to the ordinary 'everyday' explanation of behaviour may be different from that involved in stricter scientific explanations. One of the problems in the counterfactual analysis of causation has been to rule out cases where the connection is logical rather than causal. Thus the counterfactual

(11) If William had been married he wouldn't have been a bachelor

is true on the Stalnaker/Lewis account of counterfactuals, but it would not seem appropriate to say that his being unmarried causes him to be a bachelor. However, it does seem perfectly acceptable to say that because he is unmarried he is not a bachelor, and in this way the ordinary language 'because' includes the logical as well as the causal because, a fact which is nicely reflected in the counterfactual analysis.

It is a consequence of this revised analysis that the following is true:

(12) Harry took the bus because Wellington is in New Zealand and he thought the bus was going to Northampton.

Certainly (12) adds irrelevant information, but is it false? I want to say that it is true but misleading. The because clause does give sufficient reason for Harry's taking the bus, and if we rule it out because it gives too much information we run the risk of ruling out too much. A limiting case of a because explanation on this account is that every true statement is true because of the way the world is, in the sense of being entailed by the proposition which is true exactly at the world in question. I very much doubt whether there is any semantic way of drawing the line, and for that reason would leave it up to pragmatics to say when a because sentence is appropriately helpful. Nevertheless, if there should turn out to be a semantically viable way of drawing the line, little that I am going on to say would be affected.

Unfortunately, as Ed Gettier pointed out to me, the suggested revision is too broad. For it would make the following true:

(13) Harry took the bus because Wellington is in New Zealand.

This is so because 'Wellington is in New Zealand' entails 'either Wellington is in New Zealand or the bus was going to Northampton or the bus was going to Sunderland', and if the whole disjunction had been false then Harry would not have taken the bus.

So there is unfinished business for the counterfactual analysis of **because**, just as there is for Lewis's counterfactual analysis of cause. In commenting on some of the material in this chapter Lewis produced some other cases in which some revision might need to be made. To call it unfinished business is merely to remark that a direct analysis of **because** in terms of the similarity relation used in the semantics of counterfactuals may be a little too simple. After all, such an account merely trades a primitive **because** for a primitive similarity relation. What *is* illuminating is to shew that the semantics of **because**, even if we elect to take **because** as primitive, is close enough to the similarity analysis of counterfactuals to inherit the explanatory power of the latter in explaining human behaviour.

I hope it is obvious that this type of causal explanation cannot be captured by what is often called the 'covering law' model of causation. On *that* model (9) would be accounted for by saying that there is some kind of law of the form

(14) $\forall x(x$ thinks the bus is going to Northampton $\supset x$ takes the bus)

from which (9) may be deduced by universal instantiation. But of course there is no such law as (14). For instance it is only those who want to go to Northampton who would take a bus because they thought it was going there, and only those who want to go by bus, and who don't have better reasons for going elsewhere, and so on. So (14) must be replaced by

(15) $\forall x(C(x)$ & x thinks the bus is going to Northampton $\supset x$ takes the bus)

where C is a statement of the conditions which must be satisfied before we may deduce the consequent from the antecedent. Example (15) recalls pre-Stalnaker analyses of the counterfactual, and the problem was always that there seemed no way of getting the right C. What the possible-worlds account does is avoid the need for such a C. For the truth of (3) in a world w depends on getting a world as close as possible to w. In the case of (10) this means that we are entitled to take account of Harry's actual situation. If Harry wants to go to Northampton then this fact about the actual world will constrain the kind of world which is nearest to it but in which Harry thinks that the bus is not going to Northampton. Of course those who want to use a covering law model of causation may well say that it is not to be expected that statements like (9) are subject to a law as they stand. Rather it is laws of nature which underlie our reliance on counterfactuals. In fact I am happy to accept this, and nothing I have said prevents nearness from supervening on such laws, since inductive reliability could well be held to supervene on such laws.

Whether one event causes another in a world will, on the counterfactual analysis, depend on the originally given world, and no limits can be set on what features of that world may be relevant to deciding what counts as the nearest world in which the antecedent is true. Adapting a terminology derived from Putnam (1975, p. 137), and used by Jerry Fodor (see Fodor 1980, p. 244), we may say that the counterfactual analysis of causation makes it *wide* rather than narrow. Putnam uses these terms to mark a distinction between *states*. A mental state is narrow if it is preserved by molecule-for-molecule duplicates. Fodor thinks that the mental states which occur in the explanation of behaviour must be narrow because he thinks that causation is narrow; and his reason for thinking that causation is narrow is, as far as I can tell, that he adopts a covering law model of causation and such a law ought not to refer to features extraneous to the organism whose behaviour it is explaining. I do not wish to dispute that there might be a science of the mind which can be stated in terms of strict causal laws which refer only to narrow states. But neither am I committed to such a science since I shall try to shew that the ordinary explanations in terms of beliefs and desires are not this kind. Examples are not difficult to come by:

(16) Douglas entered the house because Desirée told him there was baklava inside.

It is surely clear that a molecule-for-molecule duplicate of Desirée telling Douglas that there was baklava in the house will not count as such a telling if Desirée is speaking a language in which the sentence which she utters, and which actually means that there is baklava in the house, does not mean that there is baklava in the house.

Belief/desire explanations have another feature which the counter-factual analysis easily explains, but which covering law explanations do not: *viz.* that they are intensional in not allowing replacement of co-referential singular terms. This is a point noticed by Mellor 1987 and Crane and Mellor 1990 and can be illustrated by the following example.

(17) The parcel was delivered on time because Jane believed it was urgent.

Suppose the parcel was supposed to be delivered, and was delivered, at 4.00 p.m. so its being delivered on time and its being delivered at 4.00 p.m. are one and the same event. Even so, from (17) it does not follow that

(18) The parcel was delivered at 4.00 p.m. because Jane believed it was urgent.

In this respect I am diverging slightly from Lewis's analysis, since Lewis is concerned to define event causation as in (2) via sentences to the effect that some event occurs. The problem is then how to respond to the difference between (17) and (18). Defenders of event causation can make two replies. One is that the parcel's being delivered on time and its being delivered at 4.00 p.m. are really different events and the fact that (18) does not follow from (17) shews this. I would prefer to see this reply as choosing to apply the word 'event' to what are more naturally called facts or propositions. For such a construal of events sits perfectly happily with the counterfactual analysis. On that analysis the closest world in which the parcel was not delivered on time need not be the closest world in which it was not delivered at 4.00 p.m.

The other thing a defender of event causation might say is that (18) does not follow from (17) because neither of these are true causal statements. I have already said that there may well be a stricter sense of causality operating in scientific laws according to which (17) and (18) are not causal statements. But my interest is in whatever kind of explanation is involved in (17) and (18). My own inclination is to think that causation is not a scientific notion at all, and does not play any role in scientific laws, but only in statements like (17) and (18). But that is no part of my present claim. If there is a stricter notion of causation I'll call it narrow causation, and the kind involved in (17) and (18) I'll call wide causation. This is compatible with the view that only wide causation is genuine, or the view that only narrow causation is genuine, or the view that both are genuine. The counterfactual analysis of causation makes it clear that intensionality enters right at the bottom level as part of the natural world. So whatever problems still surround the establishing of content, explaining its intensional nature is not one of them.

Whatever we decide about the terminology it should be fairly clear that it is explanations of the kind involved in (17) and (18) which are operative in our commonsense 'psychology', and it is the success of this psychology that makes Fodor link propositional attitudes and semantics with the causal explanation of behaviour. If I am right the causation involved must be wide.

Nothing I have said in this chapter of course gives any kind of analysis of just how the set of worlds which constitutes the content of a belief or desire enters into the explanation of the subject's behaviour. I believe it is a non-trivial task to do this. Nor have I said anything about how to solve all the hard problems about causal theories of representation, problems like the problem of error. Nor have I given a detailed analysis of the connections between counterfactuals and reliability. Nevertheless I hope to have given some reason to believe that the possible-worlds account of counterfactuals is the right account for commonsense causal explanations, and that the connection between nearness of worlds and reliability gives this kind of cause both practical success and evolutionary explanatoriness, and therefore a foundation for a teleological account of content; and finally and perhaps most importantly, that it provides a naturalistic account of intensionality which makes plausible the success of possible-worlds semantics.

9

Belief–desire psychology

In chapter 8 I argued that the possible-worlds account of causation provided the right model for our everyday explanation of behaviour in terms of beliefs and desires. If possible-worlds semantics is to be justified in the manner advocated by Lewis, as discussed in chapter 7 above, by reducing semantic facts to facts about belief and other propositional attitudes, then it will be necessary to reduce facts about propositional attitudes to facts which do not make reference to content. Both Lewis (1986a, pp. 27–40), and Stalnaker (1984 chapter 1) advocate the reduction of the content of attitudes via belief–desire psychology. Stalnaker contrasts what he calls the *pragmatic* picture, whereby the ascription of possible-worlds content to attitudes is made directly in terms of the role of beliefs and desires in explaining behaviour, with what he calls the *linguistic* picture, whereby the content of attitudes is explained via the content of sentences or sentence-like objects. The linguistic picture is best represented for Stalnaker in Field 1978, so before I discuss the pragmatic picture I shall look at what Field has to say, and what Stalnaker thinks of it.

Field's analysis of

(1)   *x* believes that *p*

is a conjunctive one. He supposes that when you believe something you are related to a sentence *S* (or, as he later amends the account, to some kind of representation) which means that *p*. He calls the relation to *S* belief★ and the analysis of (1) is

(2)   There exists *S* such that
      (a) *x* believes★ *S*
      (b) *S* means that *p*

Initially he accepts that *p* is a proposition in the sense of a set of possible worlds. The problem of analysing belief then becomes the two

128

subproblems of analysing (a) and (b). Of course the analysis that Field has in mind can't involve either intentional notions or semantic ones. He thinks (a) is no problem.

I believe★ a sentence of my language if and only if I am disposed to employ that sentence in a certain way in reasoning, deliberating and so on.

Although Field acknowledges the vagueness of this he thinks materialists should find it unproblematic. I have to admit that I side here with Stalnaker's worry (Stalnaker 1984, p. 28) that belief★ surely does involve semantic notions. I think that the reason why Field supposes that it does not is that if you think of believing as like saying, then you ought to be able to identify the production of a sentence token without any reference to its meaning. But even if believing is analysed as having a sentence in your 'belief box' I find it difficult to see how you can identify which box that is without invoking semantic facts. (Lynne Baker has also made this point.)

Field's principal attention is turned on (b) and here he makes use of his work on Tarski. The upshot of my discussion of that was to agree that Field had shewn that *if* you could produce an adequate account of what makes each symbol mean what it does for a given population then you have an adequate account of what all complex expressions mean. Field suggests that this problem can be solved by a causal theory of meaning. We now recall that Field is only discussing the languages of the lower predicate calculus. Nevertheless, he thinks that in analysing a belief it is not sufficient to know the extension of a predicate in the actual world - you have to know its extension in other possible worlds. He solves this by pointing out that the only access we have to knowledge of extensions is by the properties that determine them, and properties determine extensions in all worlds. So predicates have the meanings they do because they are causally related to properties.

Stalnaker (1984, p. 34) points out, in discussing Field 1972, how vague and programmatic the causal theory of reference really is. In particular, he claims that it involves intentional notions and therefore does not effect a reduction of the required sort. He also points out that a causal theory of meaning in fact involves representation at the sentence level since (p. 35) 'representation of an object is always essentially representation of it as being a certain way'. I regard this point as crucial, and would in fact go further, as I did in chapter 8, in claiming that the notion of causality relevant to establishing meaning is an intensional notion analysed using the possible-worlds semantics for counterfactuals. Stalnaker points out on page 18 that the meanings of all predicates, not just natural-kind predicates, are what they are in view of causal connections, because 'representation is essentially a causal relation'. What he rejects of course is Field's atomistic picture, where the meaning of single symbols can be causally determined. On page 35 Stalnaker says that 'one cannot separate the question "How does a name denote an object?" from the question "How does a sentence containing a name say something about the object named?"'. Stalnaker's view of Tarski's contribution is that it is in fact dealing with a different problem from the problem of naturalizing meaning. To say what the linguistic facts are that constitute a linguistic expression's having the meaning that it does in a certain speech community is derivative upon saying what the sentences of that community's language mean. Tarski's method does not answer that question. It answers the question of how speakers are able to use a language in such a way that their behaviour determines meanings for infinitely many whole sentences, most of which are never uttered.

Section II of Field's paper (pp. 24–36) is difficult. The point that Field is making is this. To call belief a *functional* relation is just to say that when I believe p today it could be because I am related to p by some relation R. When you believe p, or when I believe it tomorrow, it could be because I am related to p by some other relation R'. So a functional account of belief would only be able to avoid linguistic entities if R and R' could.

But Field has earlier argued (p. 24) that he has no idea what such a relation could look like if it did not involve representations, and so functionalism cannot do without them either. If no alternative account is possible for belief then no alternative account is possible for each of the R's that realize belief on particular occasions. I think Field is right here, but I think that a parallel distinction can be made to Stalnaker's distinction between what it is to speak a particular language and how we are able to do it. The functionalist account of what it is to believe something does not make any commitment to internal representations. But of course if you think, as Field does, that internal representations are the only account we have of how we can stand in the relations that the functionalist theory requires, then *that* fact is unaffected by the functionalist account of belief. I see no reason for Stalnaker or Lewis to doubt this, despite Field's claim on page 31 that nearly all functionalists oppose his conclusion.

But why should Field think that you can only be related to an abstract entity via a representation? Stalnaker's examples seem to shew quite clearly that you need not. One of his examples is the relation between a person and a number expressed by 'x weighs n pounds'. For this to be true no 'representation' of n inside x is required. Or, if you want a relation between a person and a proposition, Stalnaker asks us to consider the relation of need. 'x needs p' is to be true in a world w iff x would not survive unless p were true. Propositions being sets of worlds, Stalnaker plausibly points out that this relation doesn't require a representation of p inside x.

Although I think that Stalnaker is right in general, and although it may well be that representations are not required in the logical analysis of beliefs and other attitudes, yet it is not difficult to see why relations between people and propositions frequently are mediated if we look at why representations are needed. In fact doing so may provide a clue to what representation *is*. I'm going to ask why an organism might *need* to represent things. Suppose that an organism O is sensitive to rain and needs to protect itself against it. So, if it is going to rain, O should take an umbrella. But, of course, the rain is in the future, and it is usually supposed that in no genuine sense can a future event cause a past event. What is needed is a present surrogate for the future rain, which causes O to take an umbrella.

Let me call this process surrogate causation. In this sense the future rain 'causes' the present umbrella taking, but it does so only by the agency of its present surrogate. This fact of course in no sense gives an analysis of what it is for one thing to represent another, but it does make clear, at least if the last chapter convinced you that explanations in terms of the content of attitudes involve a sense of 'cause' (or of 'because') in which its terms are propositions in the sense of sets of worlds, how there could be a relation between a representation (perhaps itself construed as a proposition, say that a certain, external or internal, linguistic event occurs) and the proposition it represents.

So much for the linguistic picture. Does the pragmatic picture fare any better? If the arguments of chapter 8 are accepted then there certainly does seem *some* connection between the content of attitudes and the explanation of behaviour. If I am thirsty and believe that there is juice in the refrigerator then in some sense my thirst (i.e., presumably, my desire to drink) and my belief together conspire to get me to the refrigerator; and if that is all that the pragmatic picture is supposed to tell us then one can hardly take exception to it, certainly I shan't. For this reason I shall not attempt, and indeed am not in a position to attempt, to survey the literature on the general issue of the ascription of content to attitudes on the basis of belief/desire psychology. The semantically important question, as I see it, is whether one can formulate the pragmatic view with sufficient precision to enable the establishment of a possible-worlds content for beliefs and desires, and I shall restrict myself to discussing the attempts by Stalnaker and Lewis to do just that.

It is not to be expected of course that we shall be able to formulate a completely worked-out theory, nor need we worry that there may be a large amount of indeterminacy involved. Nevertheless one would like to have some indication of how one might go about putting together a system of beliefs and desires, in possible-worlds terms, on the basis of behaviour.

Suppose I want a drink of milk and believe that there is milk in the refrigerator. That will make it likely that I shall go to the refrigerator. So my going to the refrigerator may be part of what constitutes my having that belief and that desire. But we must be careful. Suppose I also believe that the milk has been in the refrigerator for a fortnight. Then I may well *not* go to the refrigerator. But suppose I know that it is long-life milk which will keep for a fortnight. Then maybe I *will* go to the refrigerator. And so it goes on. The point of course is that even if one's desires are held fixed, how one behaves depends on the totality of one's beliefs. A problem that Lewis and Stalnaker both recognize is that an attribution of beliefs on the basis of behaviour depends also on an attribution of desires, and that we may have no independent way of attributing desires. So that the same behaviour which justifies one set of belief ascriptions given one set of desires, could equally justify another set of beliefs given another set of desires. I shall not deal with this extra indeterminacy, since I believe that there are problems enough even if we somehow have access to a set of desires.

Assume then that, for a given agent at a given time, the agent's set of desires is specified. The account of belief attribution given in Stalnaker 1984, p. 15, is (my numbering):

(3) To believe that *P* is to be disposed to act in ways that would tend to satisfy one's desires (whatever they are) in a world in which *P* (together with one's other beliefs) were true.

It is not clear that Stalnaker is offering (3) as a *definition* of belief. He is certainly aware of the threat of circularity in defining belief in terms of desire and desire in terms of belief. I shall say more about the problem of circularity later but I shall first shew that even if understood simply as a statement of equivalence (3) is too strong. To see this I shall set out (3) a little more explicitly. (I owe this formulation to Ed Gettier who, along with Phil Bricker, suggested many moves in the ensuing argument.)

(4) X believes that P in a world w_1 iff X is disposed in w_1 to act in ways that would tend to satisfy what X desires in w_1 in a world w_2 in which P together with X's other beliefs is true.

So suppose X is a believer; i.e. suppose that for some proposition P,

(5) In w_1 X believes that P.

One difficulty about (4) lies in the phrase 'a world'. It might mean *any* world in which P together with X's other beliefs is true. Or perhaps it means the nearest world to w_1 in which this is so. But whatever it means, if in w_1 X believes that P there will have to be some world w_2 such that

(6) (i) X is disposed in w_1 to act in ways that would satisfy in w_2 what X desires in w_1, and
(ii) P, together with X's other beliefs, is true in w_2.

Since P is one of X's beliefs (6ii) entails

(6) (iii) X's beliefs are true in w_2.

Now consider the proposition $\{w_2\}$ – i.e. the proposition (set of worlds) true at w_2 and w_2 alone. From (6i) and (6iii) we have

(7) (i) X is disposed in w_1 to act in ways that would satisfy in w_2 what X desires in w_1, and
(ii) $\{w_2\}$, together with X's other beliefs, is true in w_2.

Now the *only* world that can count as a world in which $\{w_2\}$ is true is w_2. So, whatever 'a world' means in (4), from (7) by (4) we obtain

(8) X believes that $\{w_2\}$.

But to believe $\{w_2\}$ requires that X have an opinion on every proposition. As far as X is concerned there is only one way the world could be. It must be w_2. Now Stalnaker is perfectly happy to accept that agents are so rational that they accept the logical consequences of their beliefs, but it is quite another, and far less plausible, matter to rule out the logical possibility of a proposition about which a believer has no opinion. And the matter is even worse if there is more than one world which satisfies the condition stated in (6). For suppose both w_2 and w_3 satisfy (6). Then we may argue to the fact that X believes both $\{w_2\}$ and $\{w_3\}$ and therefore has incompatible beliefs. And while an agent may perhaps *have* incompatible beliefs, the argument from (4) is not a reason to attribute them.

But in fact the way Stalnaker eventually proceeds - and it is also the way Lewis (1986a, pp. 27–40) proceeds - is a little different. In place of a direct definition of what it is to believe a particular proposition we introduce the notion, familiar from modal logic, of an 'accessibility' relation between worlds, of the kind introduced on page 27 for the semantics of *possibly*. Instead of a relation of relative possibility between worlds we have a relation of 'doxastic alternativeness'. Such relations were investigated as early as Hintikka 1962. The idea is that for each person X at a time there is a relation R between worlds such that w_1Rw_2 iff w_2 is a world compatible with everything that X believes in w_1.

Given a doxastic alternativeness relation R and taking a proposition as a class of possible worlds, we say that

(9) X believes P (at t) iff for every w_2 such that w_1Rw_2, $w_2 \in P$.

This means that X believes P iff P is true in all worlds compatible with what X believes. Example (9) may seem circular and indeed might well be so if the *only* access we had to R was as a world in which all of X's beliefs are true. One way of using (3) is to see it as leading to a definition of R. Thus for any worlds w_1 and w_2,

(10) w_1Rw_2 iff X in w_1 is disposed to act in a way that would satisfy in w_2 what X desires in w_1.

I am not sure just how successful such an attempt is to *define* belief in terms of desire but at least it escapes the problems that (3) as stated has. In any case an explicit definition of R is not the only way of proceeding. An alternative is to take this relation between worlds as primitive in a theory whose testable consequences are in the behaviour predicted. Desire is treated similarly. In this case we have another relation, call it $R^\star$, such that $w_1R^\star w_2$ iff w_2 is a world in which X's desires are realized.

These accounts are oversimplified in ways that Stalnaker and Lewis are aware of. People's beliefs and desires may come in different compartments. You may believe things which are contradictory because part of you believes p and part of you believes not-p. Thus Stalnaker (1984, p. 69) speaks of belief states. Where before we had an accessibility relation which was dependent on an agent at a time, it could now happen that the very same agent can simultaneously be in more than one belief state, and it would be each belief state that is to be analysed by its own accessibility relation. Another problem is beliefs you may have about things or about yourself. You may recall the story of Uriah, whom David had killed because he wanted Bathsheba, Uriah's wife. Nathan told David a story of a man who had done what David had done. David said such a man should die. Nathan said, 'Thou art the man.' The extra sentence didn't add any new *propositions* to David's knowledge – it didn't further close off the worlds compatible with his knowledge. It merely located him, David, in one of these worlds. (See Lewis 1979a.) I shan't have anything to say here about any of these problems. The problem I shall consider is how to get empirical access to R and R★.

Lewis (1986a, p. 37) invites us to consider a person waving. In the real world, call it $w^\star$, a waves. a's waving is to be explained by a's wanting the world to be a certain way, and believing that waving would lead to its being that way. So a believes that if a were to wave the world would be one in which a's desires are realized. Combine together the analysis of belief using R, desire using R★ and counterfactuals using nearness, and Lewis's example can be expressed as

(11) If $w^\star R w_1$, then where w_2 is the closest world to w_1 in which a waves, $w_1 R^\star w_2$.

Suppose that a waves in $w^\star$. Then, says Lewis (p. 37), 'to that extent the system of belief and desire in question is a system that fits his behaviour'.

The account of desire that both Lewis and Stalnaker are assuming is that of a set of worlds in which one's desires are realized. And if we look at Lewis's analysis we see that for the hand waving to count as evidence for a particular ascription of beliefs and desires a must believe that if a were to wave then a's desires would be realized. But in fact it is never the case that there is a single action that we can perform that will realize all our desires, or if there is it happens so occasionally as to be irrelevant to the invocation of beliefs and desires in a general explanation of behaviour. Presumably what is required is some sort of ordering of worlds so that if a were to wave the world would be more desirable for a than if a were not to wave. If so then I suppose the idea would be this. Given a preference ordering of worlds and a similarity relation over worlds our aim is to arrive at a's belief worlds. We might begin with the view that any world could be one of a's belief worlds, and the aim is to narrow down this set. So, given a world w are we to throw it out? Well, on Lewis's picture the following would seem to be a sufficient condition for doing so. If $w^\star$ is the closest world to *w* in which *a* waves, and if *w*★ is better than any world in which *a* does not wave, then if *a* does not wave in *w*, *w*★ is not one of *a*'s belief worlds in *w*.

Maybe something like this would work, though it seems to me that whatever world we pick, unless it is one of the worlds which realizes all of *a*'s desires, if it is a waving world there will almost certainly be *some* better non-waving world, and if it is a non-waving world there will almost certainly be *some* better waving world. For that reason it seems likely that there will be no real-life occasions on which we are presented with a *w*★ that we can test against behaviour. So in my view a great deal more work will need to be done before it can be made plausible that belief–desire psychology gives us a way in to the content of propositional attitudes. In the next chapter (p. 150) I shall offer a rather different account of the role of belief which will be intended to shew why it is unreasonable to expect to have it play any serious role in a causal explanation of behaviour.

In discussing the views of Stalnaker in particular, though similar comments apply to Lewis as well, I have had to treat propositions as sets of worlds, with the consequence that logically equivalent propositions - being the same set of worlds - are identical. This is not just an accident of the pragmatic picture, but is essential to it. For if you analyse attitudes via counterfactuals, and if you accept Lewis's account of counterfactuals, and if any explanation of behaviour relies on accessibility relations then propositions will end up being just sets of worlds (or functions from worlds to truth values or what have you).

By contrast, if you accept the linguistic picture propositions could well be structured entities whose simple constituents are the intensions of the symbols in the sentence (or sentence-analogue) which represents the proposition. Thus the meaning of

(12) **Adriane runs**

discussed as (8) on page 22 might be not simply the set of worlds in which Adriane runs, as it would be for Stalnaker, but the structure

(13) ⟨Adriane, ω⟩

where Adriane is the person, not her name, and ω is the function from any *a* in its domain to the set of worlds in which *a* runs. In Cresswell 1985a I argued that the semantics of propositional attitudes requires structured meanings, and so the question is whether that fact requires us to use the linguistic picture rather than the pragmatic picture. What I shall do in the remainder of this chapter is detail what I believe to be the only response available to Stalnaker to the problem of logical equivalence in defending the pragmatic picture. I shall remain neutral on whether the response is adequate.

The issue concerns the question of whether you can have two propositions *p* and *q* which are logically equivalent but one is believed while the other is not. If you can, then of course *p* and *q* cannot be just sets of worlds, since they would be the same set of worlds. It should be clear that different structures could well end up evaluating to the same set of worlds, and indeed all mathematically true propositions would be the same. I shall use an example from my review, Cresswell 1988, of Stalnaker 1984. Consider

(14) The Egyptians believed that π is irrational
(15) The Egyptians believed that 2 + 2 = 4.

We can take it that (15) is certainly true, and I think we may safely assume that (14) is false. Yet

(16) π is irrational
(17) 2 + 2 = 4

being both truths of mathematics express for Stalnaker the very same proposition. Stalnaker's response to this problem is to claim that mathematical beliefs are about sentences. For the set of worlds in which (16) expresses a truth will be different from the set of worlds in which (17) does. However, we have to be careful here since what a sentence expresses is relative to an interpretation and if we treat an interpretation as a ⟨W,D,V⟩ triple, as in chapter 1, then the fact that (16) expresses a necessary truth according to ⟨W,D,V⟩ will itself, if true, be necessary. What Stalnaker must mean, when applied to (14), is something like

(18) The Egyptians believed that 'π is irrational' expressed in their language a true proposition.

But this will not do since the ancient Egyptians almost certainly had no beliefs about the sentence 'π is irrational'. Perhaps it is like this,

(19) The Egyptians believed that the sentence which for them expressed the proposition that π is irrational expressed a truth.

The problem is that for Stalnaker the proposition that π is irrational is just the proposition that 2 + 2 = 4, since both are the set of all worlds, but we certainly don't want to allow the substitution in (19), for then (14) and (15) would get the same analysis, yet one is true and the other is false.

Assuming that propositions have structure we can analyse (14) as:

(20) The Egyptians believed the proposition a which consists of the following set of worlds: $w \in a$ iff there is a sentence (appropriately close) to a sequence $\langle\alpha,\Phi\rangle$ such that, where $\langle W,D,V\rangle$ models the language spoken by the Egyptians, $V(\alpha) = \pi$ and $V(\Phi)$ is the function ω whose domain is the set of real numbers, and where for any such number r, and world w', $w' \in \omega(r)$ iff r is irrational.

The 'believed' used in (20) may be analysed in terms of a doxastic alternativeness relation. This does not mean that the verb **believe** has to be so analysed. The meaning of the word **believe** can be analysed so as to relate a person and a structure in the following way:

(21) $w \in V(\textbf{believe})(a,b)$ iff, for any world $w^\star$ which is one of a's doxastic alternatives to w, there is a sentence α such that, where $\langle W', D', V'\rangle$ models the language spoken by a in $w^\star$, α is isomorphic to b, and for any simple symbol δ in α, $V'(\delta) = d$, where d is the element of b which corresponds to δ.

What this means is simply that what we believe is a structure, but that to 'believe' a structure is to be related to a certain set of worlds, though not normally the set of worlds in which the structure is true, via a doxastic alternativeness relation.

A number of comments on this are in order. First, for the purposes of semantics it is sufficient that there *be* such a function as $V(\textbf{believes})$ even if the account of it offered in (21) is not quite right. In fact I have considerably oversimplified in assuming that a has a belief about a sentence isomorphic to b. In (20) I said 'appropriately close', and there could be some latitude on how far the surface form of the sentence might be allowed to vary. Second, it is possible to generalize (21) in a way that allows α to have more structure than b. In the limiting case b could be just a set of worlds and then $V(\textbf{believe})$ would be the 'ordinary' meaning, in terms of doxastic alternatives. These issues are discussed in more detail in Cresswell 1985a. (See especially the semantics of indirect discourse given there in chapters 12 and 13.)

Example (21) does of course make reference to the language spoken by a, and we certainly have to be careful to avoid the self-reference problems discussed in chapter 12 of Cresswell 1985a. It might be thought that (21) offends against Stalnaker's advocacy of the pragmatic picture in that it makes reference to sentences. However, Stalnaker's analysis is that unlike ordinary beliefs mathematical beliefs *are* about sentences. Example (21) is only required when the 'direct' analysis won't work. In fact Stalnaker on page 39 quotes approvingly a passage in which Richard Grandy (Grandy 1982, p. 331) argues that the vast majority of our beliefs are expressed only in linguistic behaviour, and it is in these cases that the behaviour itself involves structured entities. If this is so then it need come as no surprise that the semantics of belief might involve structured meanings.

10

Direct knowledge

In previous chapters various procedures have been discussed for reducing semantic facts about public languages to facts about propositional attitudes, and facts about propositional attitudes to physical facts. In all cases there seemed a large amount of underdetermination. Some of those who advocated these reductions, David Lewis in particular, have acknowledged this and are prepared to live with it. While I have no conclusive arguments that the amount of underdetermination is too great to be acceptable I am impressed with the difference between how little these theories deliver and how definite we seem able to be about what a person's propositional attitudes are and about what the expressions mean in the language they speak. How can this be?

One feature of the views we have looked at is that they all seem to be reductive. Thus, for Lewis, an interpreted language $\mathscr{L}$ is the language of a population P in w iff a convention of truthfulness and trust obtains in w in accordance with $\mathscr{L}$ among members of P. And belief is defined in terms of a theory that explains behaviour. The question I want to raise is this. Suppose that there is a complex pattern of behaviour which constitutes a's believing that p. Why should we expect that there should be any theory in which 'believes' is a theoretical term whose meaning is defined by the physical consequences of the theory? Suppose the behaviour of a, and facts about a's environment, perhaps including facts about other people, is so complex that no theory can describe it. Maybe this is just a practical limitation, or maybe no physical language can provide a finite description of the behaviour. The 'theories' we have referred to may give some clues as to the *kind* of behaviour that is relevant, but they cannot define what constitutes belief.

Why should it have been felt necessary that we have a *theory* of what constitutes belief? The only reason I can think of is that we can *know* what we and others believe, and if we had no theory of what belief was such knowledge would be impossible. But this seems to me to demand too much. Recall the distinction I made on pages 116–18 taken over from chapter 11 of Cresswell 1990 between supervenience and reduction. I imagined a complex organism being receptive to a very complicated pattern; a pattern too complicated for the organism to express in the physical language in which it describes the world. Since it is sensitive to this complex pattern there is no reason why it cannot have a word for it in its language. Not of course in its bottom-level physical language but in the language it actually uses when talking about ordinary everyday things.

One might describe the sensitivity as having direct acquaintance with the complex condition. There has been a resurgence of interest recently in theories of direct acquaintance, and I shall rely here on some of this work, especially some points made in Burge 1988. One point that is made is that knowledge by direct acquaintance need not be infallible. This is important because historically things known by direct acquaintance were supposed to be the building blocks out of which the world was made, and it was their certainty which justified all our knowledge of everything else. Discussion of direct acquaintance has considered, among other things, our knowledge of our own beliefs and our other intentional states. The problems that Burge is interested in may be stated using Putnam's twin-earth examples. $Oscar_1$ believes that water is wet. On one way of taking Putnam, $Oscar_1$'s belief is the belief that H_2O is wet. $Oscar_2$ is in just the same state as $Oscar_1$ but *he* believes that XYZ is wet. Since neither $Oscar_1$ nor $Oscar_2$ know about H_2O or XYZ then it would seem that neither of them can know what they believe. So it would seem that they cannot have direct acquaintance of what they believe. Burge's claim is that $Oscar_1$ does know that he believes that water is wet, and the demand that to do this, he must know the chemical composition of water is an unreasonable sceptical demand.

Knowledge by direct acquaintance is frequently thought proper only of our own mental states, and Heil 1988 prefers to speak simply of direct knowledge since he characterizes this as knowledge 'not based on evidence' (p. 239). Thus a botanist may know directly that a certain shrub is a Toyon, while I may have to infer it from other features of the shrub. None of these authors however has used direct acquaintance as a way of specifying content. Presumably being a Toyon has a botanical definition – it is simply that the botanist can directly recognize a shrub as being one. Others may know the definition and be able to infer that it is one, while others may not know the definition at all. Presumably the botanist does know the definition, but the moral of Heil's discussion is that there could be someone who could know directly that a shrub is a Toyon but who does not know the definition. The difference between the Toyon or water cases and the cases which interest me is that in the former cases there is a definition to be had whereas in the latter cases there is not. Thus, while my or another's believing that p is something that I and others can have direct knowledge of, there need be no reason to suppose that a reductive account can be given of what it is to believe that p. The fact that there is no definition to be had should not imply that one cannot have evidence for inferring that someone believes something. To suppose that would be to make the mistake I attributed to Schiffer on page 89 of thinking that a property which had to be taken as primitive could not stand in logical relations with other properties.

If direct knowledge is not limited to our own mental states then the possibility arises that we may have direct entry to the kind of knowledge which constitutes knowledge of truth conditions of the kind suggested in Cresswell 1978 as forming semantic competence. Is this plausible? Well, you hear somebody say

(1) The socks are in the second drawer of the tallboy in the bedroom upstairs.

You may or may not know whether (1) has been uttered in response to a request for information, whether perhaps it is an order for you to do something, or may be uttered by someone just reminiscing. But one thing seems to me to be clear. If you are a competent English speaker you will almost certainly instantly process such a sentence and know what it would take for it to be true. If this is right then knowledge of truth conditions is direct knowledge. But what is the content of such knowledge? The point of this chapter is simply to say that that is not a question to which there has to be an answer. When we hear others speaking our language we know directly that they are doing it. Maybe what we know directly is that they are operating with a convention which relates their linguistic behaviour with certain theoretical entities which causally explain all their behaviour. But so long as the human brain is capable of recognizing this complex pattern it does not matter whether or not we have a theory that expresses it in physical terms.

In previous chapters we saw that there was a dispute between those who, like Lewis and Stalnaker, support the view deriving from the work of Grice that public meaning depends on propositional attitudes, and those who like Field follow Fodor and others in supposing that you can only make sense of propositional attitudes if you think of them as being realized in some language-like system. Although my sympathies came down slightly on the Lewis/Stalnaker side, there are certainly arguments on both sides. If we take the direct-knowledge idea seriously and wonder how we can have direct knowledge of the attitudes of others it is certainly plausible to think that the linguistic expression of these attitudes provides a situation in which we might have such direct insight. It has been remarked (Heil 1988) that we can sometimes be more certain about the *content* of an attitude than about which particular attitude is involved. Thus while I might be unsure whether I, or you, really *believe* that *p* or whether it isn't just wishful thinking, it might be quite clear that it is *p* and not some other proposition which the unclear attitude has as its content. If our direct knowledge of attitudes is based on our direct knowledge of their linguistic expression then it would not be surprising that our knowledge of their content might be more certain than our knowledge of just which attitude is being taken towards the content.

Actually I would not be surprised if it turned out that neither way of proceeding is more basic. It seems more likely that language and attitudes develop together. Perhaps languageless creatures can have simple attitudes, and no doubt just what the meaning of a sentence is for a linguistic population is conceptually connected with their beliefs, desires and other attitudes. This possibility is compatible with seeing both meaning and attitudes as theoretical terms, though the theory might then be a single theory relating beliefs, desires *and* meanings. If so it could not be anywhere near so simple as the theories Lewis and Stalnaker put forward. In fact my guess is that it is too complicated to formulate. The human brain appears to have the ability to jump to conclusions on the basis of very meagre evidence. Pattern recognition is an instance. The price of course is extreme fallibility, but it seems plausible that what is going on there is just what is going on when we recognize a sentence as having the truth conditions it does on the basis of a very small amount of auditory (or visual) input. When people are speaking your language you just *know* that they are.

It has been stressed by several authors that the certainty with which we can predict our own future actions far outweighs the reliability of any hypothesis made on the basis of any psychological theory. Thus Gordon 1986 sees predictions of the behaviour of others as based on pretending that they are like ourselves and using our knowledge of what we would do in similar circumstances to predict what they would do. Gordon does not offer a theory of *why* this should be so, but if we have direct knowledge of our own states, and if we accept an analysis of pretence in terms of counterfactuals, and therefore in terms of possible worlds, a nice tie-up emerges between possible-worlds semantics and a rather different attitude to folk psychology from that usually taken in cognitive science.

In chapter 8 I argued that the kind of causation involved in semantics had to be 'wide' in the sense that an organism in exactly the same internal state might have different attitudes and different causal powers when placed in a different world. In comments on this claim (in a response at the 1991 Chapel Hill colloquium) Lewis argued that a wide explanation is always incomplete, and is always supportable by a more basic narrow explanation in terms of belief–desire psychology. My aim in what follows is not so much to shew that Lewis is wrong as to shew how it could be that wide explanations in terms of the content of propositional attitudes could still work, even though what underlies them might be mechanisms which do not involve content at all. If this is so then it might be unreasonable to expect to find a reductive analysis of content ascription in terms of belief–desire psychology. Is it possible to give any kind of account, which shews how it is that a scientific causal story of the role of propositional attitudes in producing behaviour might work, and might work in a manner which clearly demands wide causation?

Consider the following example. Imagine that there is an organism O, whose behaviour is sufficiently rich that we are prepared to ascribe beliefs and desires to it. O lives in an environment in which it is important that it does not get wet. In this environment grow umbrella plants which can protect O from rain. O can be in a number of states of which we shall initially concentrate on one, S. O's environment can be in a number of conditions which include one I shall call A. When the world is in A it is very likely to rain. When the world is in any other condition it is not likely to rain. When the world is in A the umbrella plants grow in place P. They don't usually grow elsewhere. Condition A causes O to go into S. S causes O to go to P and pick what is growing there. This causation need not be infallible and O need not know what is taking place. It seems to me that being in state S plausibly counts for O as believing that it is going to rain, for in condition A it displays behaviour appropriate to the rain which is likely to follow. We are assuming that it wants to avoid rain. So understood O's belief that it will rain leads it to appropriate behaviour given its desire.

Suppose all this is true in the real world w_1. But now suppose another world w_2 in which A causes sunshine. Sunshine is just as harmful to O as rain. (O likes dry overcast weather of the sort you get in Lima for eight months of the year.) A still causes O to go into S and still causes the parasol plants to grow at P. In w_2 it is surely true that O's being in S is believing not that it is going to rain, but that it is going to be sunny. The point of this example is simply to shew how wide causation can operate in the sphere of propositional attitudes. For in world w_1 it is certainly true that if O had not believed that it was going to rain it would not have picked umbrella plants and in w_2 it is true that if O had not believed that it was going to be sunny then it would not have picked parasol plants - that is assuming that in w_1 being in S is believing that it will rain, and in w_2 being in S is believing that it will be sunny. Further, there is a perfectly good evolutionary explanation for why the same internal state constitutes different beliefs in different worlds. In w_1 organisms survive who protect themselves against rain, while in w_2 organisms survive who protect themselves against sun.

The upshot of this is simply that the sense of causality used in ordinary commonsense explanations, a sense which fits very happily into an evolutionary account of propositional attitudes, does not demand that the content of a belief supervene on the internal states of the believer. In this example the content of S depends on features of w_1 and w_2 which are external to O. In this respect it is like the twin-earth examples discussed in Fodor 1982 and in chapter 2 of Fodor 1987 and which are intended to shew that although Oscar and twin Oscar may be in the same internal state, Oscar has a belief about H_2O, while twin Oscar has a belief about XYZ. There is, however, this difference. In the twin-earth example there is supposed to be no macroscopically detectable difference between Earth and Twin-Earth. In the example I have discussed rain and sun are very different. The difference between the two examples is relevant in this respect. I have already mentioned that Fodor wants to argue that belief is a narrow state. His response to twin-earth arguments is to say that (wide) semantic content is narrow content + context. In other words there is a sense in which the belief of Oscar and twin Oscar have the same content, and it is this sense of content which is relevant to explaining their behaviour.

Such a response seems less convincing in the present example since we would have to suppose that there is a sense of content in which the narrow content of a belief that it will rain is identical with the narrow content of a belief that it will be sunny, and although there is certainly a function which takes w_1 into the set of worlds in which it will rain, and takes w_2 into the set of worlds in which it is sunny, such a function seems too attenuated to be called content in any reasonable sense. Of course Fodor may well respond that the notion of narrow content in this example is attenuated precisely because the range of behaviour that we allow to realize the belief is so restricted. If O has other beliefs about rain and sun then the states which are these other beliefs will have different internal connections with S, and will therefore shew that S is not really one state but two. Maybe this response is correct, but it is irrelevant to my use of the example, for all I want to argue is that wide causation is sufficient *whether or not* Fodor is right about narrow states. The example is intended to shew how wide content works, even if Fodor's critics are right that there is no narrow state of belief. In fact my purpose is not so much to attack Fodor as to attack the assumption that belief–desire psychology could only contribute to a causal explanation of behaviour if belief is a narrow state. If it is, so much the better, but it doesn't have to be. In fact, even this last remark goes further than I would really like to be committed to, in that I do not wish to make any claims about the scientific status of commonsense explanations in terms of beliefs and desires, and perhaps my use of the word 'psychology' is ill advised. Fodor 1991 argues that if beliefs are to figure in a scientific theory they must have 'causal powers'. Whether the role of S in O's behaviour gives it 'causal power' in Fodor's sense is an issue on which I remain neutral.

We don't actually have to move to different worlds to get the same effect. Suppose that in the actual world there are two different, and incompatible, conditions, A and B. A causes rain and causes umbrella plants to grow in P and O to go into state S. B causes sunshine and causes parasol plants to grow in Q and O to go into state S. Now the way state S works differs according as the world is in A or B. A sends sensory signals which combine with S to lead O to P while B sends signals which combine with S to lead O to Q. Since neither we, the observers, nor O need know this the claim that O believes that it will rain is not the claim that O is in S, nor is the claim that O believes that it will be sunny. And if you think that rain and sun have a common *semantic* content it would be easy to devise cases in which A and B, and P and Q, had nothing in common in any reasonable semantical sense.

Even if belief is a narrow state, it still does not follow that its role in explaining behaviour can be based on its non-semantic properties. To see this I shall adapt the original example slightly. Suppose that O can be in two states S_1 and S_2. Their nature is irrelevant except that they must be incompatible. O can never be in both. (But may be in neither.) O's environment can be in a number of conditions which include two, A_1 and A_2. (These two conditions are incompatible.) When the world is in A_1 it is very likely to rain. When the world is in A_2 it is very likely to rain. When the world is in any other condition it is not likely to rain. When the world is in A_1 the umbrella plants grow in place P_1. When the world is in A_2 the umbrella plants grow in place P_2. They don't usually grow elsewhere. Condition A_1 (A_2) causes O to go into S_1 (S_2). S_1 causes O to go to P_1 and pick what is growing there. S_2 causes O to go to P_2 and pick what is growing there. This causation need not be infallible and O need not know that that is what is taking place.

It seems to me that such a case is plausibly described by saying that O believes that it is going to rain iff O is in state S_1 in condition A_1 or is in state S_2 in condition A_2. For in those conditions it displays behaviour appropriate to protecting it from rain. O could be wrong either by being in S_1 or S_2, but with A_1 or A_2 not resulting in rain, or by A_1 or A_2 failing to cause S_1 or S_2. The question is whether there is a single state of believing that it will rain. If there is then the only candidate is the disjunctive state $S_1 \vee S_2$. But suppose that O is in S_1 while the world is in A_2. We would have to say that O mistakenly believes that it will rain. In many cases this will be the right thing to say, but I am not sure that it will be the right thing in all cases. For suppose that there is a very rare condition B, which occasionally occurs when the world is in A_2, and produces something more dangerous than rain - some kind of solar radiation. In *those* conditions the protecting plants grow in P_1 and so condition B overrides A_2 and causes O to go into S_1. Condition B, we shall say, causes O to go into S_1 by mimicking condition A_1 in the immediate environment of O. In this case I think we would not say that O mistakenly believes it will rain even though O is in $S_1 \vee S_2$. But even if $S_1 \vee S_2$ is a single 'state' that counts as a belief that it will rain, there seems no way that an examination of O's internal structure will indicate that it is a single state. All that unifies $S_1 \vee S_2$ is the fact that it causes behaviour appropriate to rain.

In this example it might be held that at the level of 'real science' what is going on is not that O exhibits certain behaviour because it believes it will rain. Rather it is that being in S_1 causes it to go to P_1 and being in S_2 causes it to go to P_2, where A_1 causes S_1 and A_2 causes S_2. When science progresses from the 'folk' level we shall have no need for the explanation in terms of beliefs. I am happy to concede all this. But this story in no way casts doubt on the practical utility of the belief–desire explanation. For neither we nor O may know about A_1 or A_2 or S_1 or S_2. Yet we can use O's behaviour as an indication of rain. Further, if you think of the evolutionary explanation for O's behaviour you will see that going to P_1 or P_2 is not important *per se*. It is only going to P_1 in condition A_1 and going to P_2 in A_2 which enables O to avoid rain. So, say if you like that that is not real science. Practical success and evolutionary explanatoriness are good enough for me.

Of course in the present case it is easy to *reduce* the belief–desire explanation to the 'real' one, by formulating it as

(2) Being in S_1 in A_1 or S_2 in A_2 causes O to go to P_1 in A_1 or P_2 in A_2 and pick what is there.

Example (2) follows from the laws about S_1, S_2, A_1 and A_2 individually, and may be regarded as the definiens for

(3) Believing that it will rain causes O to pick umbrella plants.

Yet a more realistic example may preclude such reduction. For isn't it more plausible to suppose that there are not just two conditions of the world and two states of believing that it will rain, but that there are infinitely many - or if not infinitely many at least too large a number for us to codify in any humanly comprehensible scientific laws? This would be an example of what I called in chapter 11 of Cresswell 1990 supervenience without reducibility. This point is taken up in Stalnaker 1989. There is no reason to suppose that this open-endedly large disjunction can be identified in any way other than by its semantic properties, or that the mechanisms by which the disjuncts produce the appropriate behaviour should be statable by any system of causal laws. It doesn't follow from this that they can't be so statable. Fodor presumably thinks that they are. All that is necessary is to repeat that belief–desire psychology, being based on wide causation, is not committed to such laws.

Notice that the Lewis account of causation fits perfectly happily with the situation we are describing. For consider the counterfactual

(4) If O hadn't believed it would rain then O would not have picked umbrella plants.

Example (4) is offered as an explanation of what is going on when O does believe it will rain and therefore picks umbrella plants. Now whatever is the case about a world in which O doesn't believe it will rain there are two kinds of world we know it cannot be. It cannot be a world in which O is in S_1 and conditions are A_1 and it cannot be a world in which O is in S_2 and conditions are A_2. But we have supposed that in conditions A_1 the umbrella plants grow in P_1, and O is caused to go there only when in S_1, and in conditions A_2 the umbrella plants grow only at P_2 and O is caused to go there only when in S_2. So (4) is true.

In the case of our knowledge of our own attitudes, presumably what happens is that one part of the brain is sensitive to a complex pattern occurring in another part of the brain. When this happens the belief becomes conscious, and it is this fact that enables us to refer to a belief that *p* even though we may have no account to offer of what constitutes believing that *p*. Consider the disjunctive state $S_1 \vee S_2$ which was suggested as being O's belief that it is going to rain. The point made on page 147 was that this 'state' is only unified semantically. But suppose that O's belief becomes a conscious one. Then presumably there is a metastate M which is triggered either by S_1 or by S_2 and not by any other state. Unlike the case as originally described, it now *will* be possible, by examining O's internal structure, to unify $S_1 \vee S_2$ and consider it to be a single state. If O has a language then M might be what causes it to say 'it is going to rain', and, if so, then it is likely that M will itself have a sentence-like structure. It might be that *this* is the truth behind the language-of-thought hypothesis.

I must admit to having no idea of what kind of a thing M could be which could take $S_1 \vee S_2$ as input and produce a sentence-like structure as output. As Bestor (1991, p. 306) notes, the language-of-thought model looks best when we imagine both the inputs and outputs having linguistic form, but looks less good when we imagine sensory input and motor output. In the umbrella-plant example the behaviour that S_1 causes can be quite different from the behaviour S_2 causes. This would be so if P_1 and P_2 were so different that completely different actions were required to get to each place. And of course the situation would be even worse in the real-life case where, instead of only two disjuncts, there would be many million. So $S_1 \vee S_2$ cannot *be* a sentence in a language of thought, and it is a non-trivial problem to see what kind of thing M could be to convert it into one.

In relating direct knowledge to the umbrella-plant example I have been accepting that states like S_1, S_2 or their disjunction can count as beliefs because of the causal role that they play in behaviour. But one could look at the matter in another way. If you think that the 'real' causal story about O is simply that S_1 causes it to go to P_1 and S_2 causes it to go to P_2 and that is all there is to it, you could say that $S_1 \vee S_2$ only counts as a *belief* that it is going to rain when it is recognized by M. If *this* is what beliefs do then their explanatory role will certainly be very gappy. For we shall no longer need to find a belief to explain all our rational behaviour. This doesn't mean that beliefs have no connection with the causes of behaviour. It is just that we would no longer expect to find a system of beliefs and desires to fit all our behaviour. Further, if beliefs arise only when brain states are consciously recognized it becomes entirely plausible that they be known directly, and that we can be so certain that we and others *have* beliefs, even though we may have no account to offer of just what constitutes the having of a belief. Certainly beliefs and desires wouldn't be things which are likely to play any useful role in a scientific theory, and if you thought that they had to you might even be driven to the view that there are no beliefs and desires - as indeed some theorists have been. Authors like Stich (1983), Paul Churchland (1981), and Patricia Churchland (1980) have argued for what is called an *eliminativist* view of propositional attitudes, specifically beliefs, and desires. Their arguments have the following structure:

(5) Beliefs (desires) are things that play causal role C in a (true) psychological theory.
(6) Nothing plays role C in any true psychological theory
∴(7) There are no beliefs or desires.

The purpose of this chapter has been to take issue with (5) on the ground that it is too strong. No doubt, if we are physicalists,

(8) X believes that *p*

is constituted by a collection of physical facts. No doubt also there is some real or imagined connection in the minds of ordinary folk between the truth of (8) and an explanation of why X behaves as X does. But that is far weaker than requiring 'believes' to get its meaning by being a term in a (mostly) correct psychological theory.

The problem is how we can have access to this collection of physical facts which constitute (8) and that is where direct knowledge comes in. It is not that being recognized by M is what gives S_1 V S_2 the content it does. It has that because of a connection with rain, even if it is a connection not expressed in any psychological theory. It is through M that O can have access to S_1 V S_2 and so count it as a belief. In this way it is possible to accept all the criticisms of folk psychology that the eliminativists produce without having to deny the manifest fact that we do believe things and do desire things.

References

Åqvist, L. E. G. son, 1973, Modal logic with subjunctive conditionals and dispositional predicates. *Journal of Philosophical Logic*, Vol. 2, pp. 1-26.

Barwise, J., and R. Cooper, 1981, Generalized quantifiers and natural language. *Linguistics and Philosophy*, Vol. 4, pp. 159-219.

Bestor, T. W., 1991, Naturalizing semantics: new insight or old folly. *Inquiry*, Vol. 34, pp. 285-310.

Burge, T., 1988, Individualism and self-knowledge. *The Journal of Philosophy*, Vol. 85, pp. 649-63.

Churchland, P. M., 1981, Eliminative materialism and the propositional attitudes. *The Journal of Philosophy*, Vol. 78, pp. 67-90.

Churchland, P. S., 1980, Language, thought and information. *Noūs*, Vol. 14, pp. 147-70.

Crane, T. M., and D. H. Mellor, 1990, There is no question of physicalism. *Mind*, Vol. 99, pp. 185-219.

Cresswell, M. J., 1973, *Logics and Languages*, London, Methuen.
  1978, Semantic competence. In *Meaning and Translation*, ed. F. Guenthner and M. Guenthner-Reutter, London, Duckworth, pp. 9-43 (reprinted in Cresswell, *Semantical Essays*, Dordrecht, Reidel, 1988, pp. 12-33).
  1982, The autonomy of semantics. In *Beliefs, Processes and Questions*, ed. P. S. Peters and E. Saarinen, Dordrecht, Reidel, pp. 69-86.
  1985a, *Structured Meanings*, Cambridge, Mass., MIT Press, Bradford Books.
  1985b, *Adverbial Modification*, Dordrecht, Reidel.
  1988, Review of Stalnaker 1984. *Linguistics and Philosophy*, Vol. 14, pp. 515-19.
  1990, *Entities and Indices*, Dordrecht, Kluwer.

Davidson, D., 1967, Truth and meaning. *Synthese*, Vol. 17, pp. 304-23.

Dudman, V. H., 1984, Conditional interpretations of *if*-sentences. *Australian Journal of Linguistics*, Vol. 4, pp. 143-204.

Field, H., 1972, Tarski's theory of truth. *The Journal of Philosophy*, Vol. 69, pp. 347-75.
  1978, Mental representation. *Erkenntnis*, Vol. 13, pp. 9-61.

Fodor, J. A., 1980, Methodological solipsism. In *Representations*, Brighton, Harvester Press, pp. 225-53.
  1982, Cognitive science and the twin-earth problem. *Notre Dame Journal of Formal Logic*, Vol. 23, pp. 98-118.
  1987, *Psychosemantics*, Cambridge, Mass., MIT Press.

1991, A modal argument for narrow content. *The Journal of Philosophy*, Vol. 88, pp. 5-26.

Gordon, R. M., 1986, Folk psychology as simulation. *Mind and Language*, Vol. 1, pp. 158-71.

Grandy, R. E. 1982, Semantic intentions and linguistic structure. *Notre Dame Journal of Formal Logic*, Vol. 23, pp. 327-32.

Grice, H. P., 1957, Meaning. *The Philosophical Review*, Vol. 66, pp. 377-88.

1968, Utterer's meaning, sentence-meaning and word-meaning. *Foundations of Language*, Vol. 4, pp. 225-42.

Hawthorne, J., 1990, A note on 'Languages and language'. *Australasian Journal of Philosophy*, Vol. 68, pp. 116-18.

Heil, J., 1988, Privileged access. *Mind*, Vol. 97, pp. 238-51.

Hintikka, K. J. J., 1962, *Knowledge and Belief*, Ithaca, Cornell University Press.

Kaplan, D., 1975, How to Russell a Frege–Church. *The Journal of Philosophy*, Vol. 72, pp. 716-29.

1978, Transworld heir lines. In *The Possible and the Actual*, ed. M. J. Loux, Ithaca, Cornell University Press, 1979, pp. 88-109.

1979, On the logic of demonstratives. *Journal of Philosophical Logic,* Vol. 8, pp. 81-98.

Kratzer, A. H. E. S., 1977, What 'must' and 'can' must and can mean. *Linguistics and Philosophy*, Vol. 1, pp. 113-26.

Kripke, S. A., 1972a, Naming and necessity. *Semantics of Natural Language*, ed. D. Davidson and G. Harman, Dordrecht, Reidel, pp. 253-355.

1972b, Identity and necessity. In *Identity and Individuation*, ed. M. Munitz, New York University Press.

Lewis, D. K., 1969, *Convention*, Cambridge, Mass., Harvard University Press.

1971, Counterparts of persons and their bodies. *The Journal of Philosophy*, Vol. 68, pp. 203-11.

1972, General semantics. *Semantics of Natural Language*, ed. D. Davidson and G. Harman, Dordrecht, Reidel, pp. 169-218.

1973a, *Counterfactuals*, Oxford, Basil Blackwell.

1973b, Causation. *The Journal of Philosophy*, Vol. 70, pp. 556-67 (reprinted in Lewis 1986b with Appendices).

1975, Languages and language. In *Language, Mind and Knowledge*, ed. K. Gunderson, Minneapolis, University of Minnesota Press, pp. 3-35.

1979a, Attitudes *de dicto* and *de se*. *The Philosophical Review*, Vol. 88, pp. 513-43.

1979b, Counterfactual dependence and time's arrow. *Noûs*, Vol. 13, pp. 455-76.

1984, Putnam's paradox. *Australasian Journal of Philosophy*, Vol. 62, pp. 221-36.

1986a, *On the Plurality of Worlds*, Oxford, Basil Blackwell.

1986b, Events. In *Philosophical Papers*, Vol. II, New York, Oxford University Press, pp. 241-69.

1992, Meaning without use: reply to Hawthorne. *Australasian Journal of Philosophy*, Vol. 70, pp. 106-10.

Loux, M. J. (ed.), 1979, *The Possible and the Actual*, Ithaca, Cornell University Press.

Lycan, W. G., 1979, The trouble with possible worlds. *The Possible and the Actual*, ed. M. J. Loux, Ithaca, Cornell University Press, pp. 274-316.

Mellor, D. H., 1987, The singularly affecting facts of causation. In *Metaphysics and Morality*, ed. P. Pettit *et al.*, Oxford, Blackwell (reprinted in *Matters of Metaphysics*, Cambridge University Press, 1991, pp. 201-24).

Montague, R. M., 1974, *Formal Philosophy*, New Haven, Yale University Press.

Plantinga, A., 1976, Actualism and possible worlds. *Theoria*, Vol. 42, pp. 139-60 (reprinted in Loux 1979, pp. 253-73).

Prior, A. N., and K. Fine, 1977, *Worlds, Times and Selves*, London, Duckworth.

Putnam, H., 1975, The meaning of 'meaning'. In *Language, Mind and Knowledge*, ed. K. Gunderson, Minneapolis, University of Minnesota Press, pp. 131-93 (reprinted in *Mind, Language and Reality*, Cambridge University Press, 1975, pp. 215-71).

    1977, Models and reality. Presidential Address to the Association for Symbolic Logic, December 1977. *The Journal of Symbolic Logic*, Vol. 45, 1980, pp. 464-82 (reprinted in *Realism and Reason*, Cambridge University Press, 1983, pp. 1-25).

Quine, W. V. O., 1948, On what there is. *Review of Metaphysics*, Vol. 1 (reprinted in Quine 1953, pp. 1-19).

    1953, *From a Logical Point of View*, Cambridge, Mass., Harvard University Press (revised edition 1961).

    1960, *Word and Object*, Cambridge, Mass., MIT Press.

    1969, Ontological relativity. In *Ontological Relativity and Other Essays*, New York, Columbia University Press, pp. 26-68.

Russell, B. A. W., 1905, On denoting. *Mind*, Vol. 14, pp. 479-93.

Salmon, N., 1987, Existence. In *Philosophical Perspectives*, Vol. 1 *Metaphysics*, ed. J. E. Tomberlin, Atascadero, Calif., Ridgeview, pp. 49-108.

Schiffer, S., 1987, *Remnants of Meaning*, Cambridge, Mass., MIT Press.

Soames, S., 1984, What is a theory of truth? *The Journal of Philosophy*, Vol. 82, pp. 411-29.

Stalnaker, R. C., 1968, A theory of conditionals. In *Studies in Logical Theory*, ed. N. Rescher, Oxford, Basil Blackwell, pp. 98-112.

    1978, Assertion. In *Pragmatics*, ed. P. Cole, *Syntax and Semantics*, Vol. IX, New York, Academic Press, pp. 315-32.

    1984, *Inquiry*, Cambridge, Mass., MIT Press, Bradford Books.

    1989, On what's in the head. In *Philosophical Perspectives*, Vol. III: *Philosophy of Mind and Action Theory*, ed. J. E. Tomberlin, Atascadero, Calif., Ridgeview, pp. 287-316.

Stich, S. P., 1983, *From Folk Psychology to Cognitive Science: the Case against Belief*, Cambridge, Mass., MIT Press.

Tarski, A., 1936, The concept of truth in formalized languages. In *Logic, Semantics and Metamathematics*, Oxford, Clarendon Press, 1956, pp. 152-278.

Thomason, R. H., 1976, Necessity, quotation, and truth: an indexical theory. In *Language in Focus*, ed. A. Kasher, Dordrecht, Reidel, pp. 119-38.

Index

Index

Hawthorne, J., 100, 105
Heil J., 141,
Hintikka, K.J.J., 38, 134

if, 5–7, 24, 26, 36, 50, 110
Impossible objects, 61–3
Individual essence, 64
 exemplification of, 64
Individual variable, 49
Individuals, as functions to spatio-temporal regions, 60, 67
Intended interpretation, 23, 30, 38, 110
Intension/extension distinction, 72, 110
Interpretation, ⟨W,D,V⟩ for 𝓛, 18, 23, 32
 isomorphic interpretations, 35, 36
is XYZ, 83, 141, 145
Isomorphic interpretations, 35f.
Isomorphism problem, 36, 40

Kaplan, D., 38, 42, 59, 81, 83
King of France, 62, 82
Kratzer, 1977, 27
Kripke, S.A., 31, 61, 75, 80, 110

𝓛, formal language, 5
 categorial, 8
 compositionality, 13, 98
 conventionality of, 13
 disambiguated, 12
 intended interpretation for, 23, 30, 38, 110
 interpretation ⟨W,D,V⟩ for, 18, 23, 32
 semantics for, 12–17, 20–9, 32
Lewis, D.K., 1, 3, 58, 63, 142, 144
 1969, 95
 1971, 67
 1972, 13
 1973a, 2, 115, 118
 1973b, 2, 115, 125
 1975, 2, 94–104, 108, 140
 1979a, 135
 1979b, 115, 118
 1984, 40
 1986a, 39, 65, 95, 128, 134, 135, 134–6
 1986b, 116
 1992, 105

counterpart theory, 65–8
 haecceitism, 68f.
 natural properties, 69
Linguistic picture, 128, 136
Logical possibility, 61
Logically equivalent propositions, 64, 136-9
Loux, M.J., 43, 59, 61
Löwenheim–Skolem theorem, 36
Lycan, W.G., 1979, 61
λ-abstraction, 78

M, metastate, 150
Meinong, A., 61
Mellor, D.H., 125
Metalogical variables, 6, 22
Metaphysical weakness, principle of, 70
Metaphysics
 metaphysical necessity, 75
 possible-worlds, 38, 116
Modal facts, 116
Modifier, predicate, 9
 category (s/n)/(s/n) of, 10
Montague, R.M., 8, 40, 42, 88

n, name category, 9, 11, 32
name
 in a categorial language, 5, 13, 17
 category n of, 9, 11, 32
Narrow state, 124, 145, 146
Natural properties, 69
necessarily, 91
Necessity, metaphysical, 75,
 epistemic, 75
{n:n is even}, 15
nobody, 9, 77
Non-existence-entailing predicate, 62
not, 5, 7, 24, 25f., 36, 50, 110
n-tuple, 18
ν, assignment to variables, 49
 x-alternative of ν, 50
 (ν, a/x), 78

O, occurrence predicate, 115
Occupied, 116
Ockham's razor, 70
One-place functor, 5

157

For EU product safety concerns, contact us at Calle de José Abascal, 56–1°, 28003 Madrid, Spain or eugpsr@cambridge.org.

www.ingramcontent.com/pod-product-compliance
Ingram Content Group UK Ltd.
Pitfield, Milton Keynes, MK11 3LW, UK
UKHW012341130625
459647UK00009B/445